CULTURES OF THE WORLD®

ISRAEL

Jill DuBois/Mair Rosh

BENCHMARK BOOKS

MARSHALL CAVENDISH
NEW YORK

PICTURE CREDITS
Cover photo: © Art Directors & TRIP/Adina Tovy
AFP: 17, 46 • Art Directors & TRIP: 1, 18, 40, 42, 51, 52, 72, 92, 104, 121 • Bes Stock: 9,
54 • Werner Braun: 3, 15, 29, 30, 35, 39, 43, 75, 91, 94, 103, 109, 114 • Embassy of Israel,
Singapore: 11, 22, 26, 27, 28, 31, 33 • The Image Bank: 14, 16, 41, 47, 49, 67, 71, 76, 87
• Hanan Isachar: 5, 6, 8, 24, 32, 48, 50, 53, 55, 56, 58, 63, 68, 70, 80, 82, 98, 106, 107, 108,
112, 116, 118, 120, 125, 127, 131 • Israel Images: 130 • Life Photo: 7, 34, 36, 37, 38, 44,
59, 61, 74, 86, 88, 93, 96, 97, 105, 124, 126 • Lonely Planet Images: 13, 128 • Anat Rotem-
Braun: 4, 10, 45, 62, 69, 78, 79, 100, 102, 111, 117, 123 • Jamie Simson: 19, 20, 21, 23, 25,
60, 64, 65, 66, 83, 85, 99

ACKNOWLEDGMENTS
With thanks to Jacob Lassner, professor of History and Religion, Northwestern University,
Evanston, Illinois, for his expert reading of this manuscript

PRECEDING PAGE
Jewish boys begin wearing skullcaps from an early age. Their skullcaps come in a variety
of fabrics, colors, and designs, for daily wear and for special occasions and holidays.

Marshall Cavendish Corporation
99 White Plains Road
Tarrytown, NY 10591
Website: www.marshallcavendish.com

© 1993, 2004 by Times Media Private Limited
All rights reserved. First edition 1993. Second edition 2004.

Originated and designed by
Times Books International, an imprint of
Times Media Private Limited, a member of
Times International Publishing

Printed in Malaysia

Library of Congress Cataloging-in-Publication Data
DuBois, Jill, 1952-
Israel / by Jill DuBois and Mair Rosh.— 2nd ed.
    p. cm. — (Cultures of the world)
Summary: Explores the geography, history, government, economy, people,
and culture of Israel.
Includes bibliographical references and index.
    ISBN 0-7614-1669-2
1. Israel—Juvenile literature. [1. Israel.] I. Rosh, Mair. II. Title. III. Series.
DS102.95.D82 2003
956.94—dc21   2003010083

7 6 5 4 3

CONTENTS

A Palestine sunbird drinking water.

The Jerusalem Theater.

INTRODUCTION

ISRAEL WAS ESTABLISHED IN 1948 as a modern recreation of an ancient Jewish State. A functioning democracy, this is a land considered sacred by Jews, Christians, and Muslims alike. Known for its turbulent politics and holy sites, this is also a land of contrasts. Walk the streets of the capital city Jerusalem and you will see ancient walls, shrines, and ruins next to modern office buildings, cafes, and boutiques with the latest international fashions.

Israel is a small country, about the size of Massachusetts, that has many historical, cultural, and natural attractions. Israel's citizens enjoy brilliant white beaches, three cosmopolitan cities, enchanting deserts, valleys filled with wildflowers, and a mountain-top ski resort. A modern oasis sprung from the desert, one can pray at the Western Wall, trace the steps of Jesus of Nazareth, and visit Islam's third holiest place of worship.

GEOGRAPHY

THE MODERN STATE OF ISRAEL is an ancient land that has been a nation for the Jewish people since 1948. Israel is located in the Middle East, on the eastern shore of the Mediterranean Sea. Geographically, Israel belongs to the Asian continent. It acts as a bridge connecting Asia, Africa, and Europe. Israel is bound to the north by Lebanon, to the northeast by Syria, to the east and southeast by Jordan, and to the southwest by Egypt. Israel's southernmost tip extends to the Gulf of Aqaba and the Red Sea.

Israel currently occupies some 8,000 square miles (53,679 square km), making it approximately the size of the state of Massachusetts in the United States. Israel is a long wedge of land, with its width as narrow as 10 miles (26 km) in some areas and no wider than 70 miles (181 km) at any point.

Despite its small size, Israel contains many types of geographical terrain: mountains, valleys, deserts, and forests with a rich variety of plants and animals.

Israel is the only Jewish state in the world. Its creation represents the fulfillment of a prophecy from the Bible in which God promised the land to the Jewish people, and the desire of the Jews, who wanted a nation that Jews from around the world could call home.

Modern-day Jews established themselves on Israel's coastal plain. This narrow strip is about 115 miles (185 km) long and is covered mainly by alluvial soils, which are fertile and suitable for crop cultivation.

Above: **The Mushroom Rock in the Arava Valley.**

Opposite: **Wildflowers in full bloom in the Judean Mountains during spring.**

7

TOPOGRAPHY

There are four geographic regions: hills in the northern and central regions, the western coastal plain, the Jordan Rift Valley (part of the Great Rift Valley) in the east, and the Negev Desert in the south.

There are three distinct hilly regions. The hills of Galilee to the north include the highest mountain in Israel, Mount Meron (3,963 feet, or 1,208 m). This range gets a lot of rain and has fertile valleys that produce tobacco and olives. South of the hills of Galilee is the hot and humid but fertile Esdraelon Plain, formerly a swampland. Upland plateaus lie south of the plain.

The western coastal plain is the most populated region with Tel Aviv and the principal port Haifa. This heartland of Israel has citrus plantations, planned settlements, and industries.

The Great Rift Valley is a deep depression formed millions of years ago when the floor of the Jordan river valley and the Dead Sea collapsed. It extends south approximately 274 miles (710 km) and is dominated by the Jordan River, the Sea of Galilee, and the Dead Sea.

The Negev Desert comprises more than half of Israel's total land area. It was once almost 20 percent larger than it is now, but agricultural development has decreased its size. The majority of *kibbutzim* (key-BOOT-zim) and *moshavim* (MOH-shau-vim), the agricultural settlements of Israel that exist all over Israel, are located in the Negev.

SEAS AND RIVERS

The most important river in Israel is the Jordan. It originates in the Golan Heights in the north, runs southward near the borders of Lebanon and Syria, through the Sea of Galilee, and empties into the Dead Sea. The Yarkon and the Kishon rivers are the only other waterways with permanent flows; others are dry throughout most of the year. The Yarkon runs into the Mediterranean Sea near Tel Aviv, and the Kishon does so near Haifa. Both the Jordan and the Yarkon are irrigation sources for the Negev Desert.

Above: **The Dead Sea has such a high mineral content that even a non-swimmer can float unaided on its surface.**

Opposite: **These columns at Arava in the Negev desert were part of the temple that King Solomon built in 950 B.C.**

The National Water Carrier, a freshwater pipeline system from the Sea of Galilee, provides drinking as well as irrigation water to the desert. Also known as Lake Kinneret or Tiberias, the Sea of Galilee is a very popular vacation and fishing area.

The Dead Sea is a large saltwater lake that is almost three times as salty as the Mediterranean Sea. It is 1,300 feet (396 m) below sea level, making it the lowest place on earth. Its salt content is so high that the land around it cannot be cultivated, but its water is said to have certain healing qualities.

The Dead Sea cannot sustain fish or plant life, hence its name. However, it has great commercial value as it is one of the world's largest sources of potash, as well as a plentiful source of magnesium bromide, magnesium chloride, and salt. It is also the site of the biblical cities of Sodom and Gomorrah, which were completely destroyed.

Snow in Yemim Moshe, the first settlement outside the Old City walls of Jerusalem.

CLIMATE

The climate of Israel has been characterized as Mediterranean, which means that it has two seasons: winter, which lasts from November through March, and summer, which lasts from April through October.

During summer there is little rain, and temperatures can rise well above 90°F (32°C) in some parts. Summer temperatures are higher in the desert, mountain ranges, and valleys. Nearly 70 per cent of the annual rainfall takes place during winter.

Because of Israel's location between desert and the humid Mediterranean Sea, rainfall is not evenly distributed throughout the country. In the south, the average rainfall is one-tenth that of the north. Temperatures differ from north to south as well. In summer, cool breezes prevail in Jerusalem in the north, while the desert can be as hot as 120°F (49°C).

One particularly bothersome part of Israel's weather is its windstorms. Hot desert winds that carry dust and sand can lower humidity and raise temperatures to almost unbearable levels. These windstorms happen occasionally from October to May.

FLORA AND FAUNA

There is plenty of plant life in Israel, from flowering plants to brushes and shrubs. It is believed that more than 2,000 plant species grow here, with wild flowers dotting the mountains and valleys, and cacti adorning the desert. In fact, the native Israeli is known as a Sabra, or prickly pear, named after the cactus fruit, which is tough on the outside but sweet on the inside.

Flowers are so plentiful here that the country began selling cut flowers in the 1960s, and in 20 years Israel grew into Europe's largest supplier. Tulips, roses, anemones, irises, poppies, and cyclamen are among the many blooms found in Israel.

For centuries trees covered Israel's mountains, but the demand for lumber and firewood, years of cultivation, and grazing goats and sheep, combined with erosion from the sometimes violent, cyclone-like desert storms, have destroyed much vegetation.

Deer in Hai Bar Park on Mount Carmel.

However, there has been a successful and aggressive reforestation program underway for many decades. Millions of trees have been planted under the program. Species of trees and brush that do survive are Aleppo pines and Tabor and evergreen oaks. Almond and fruit trees such as olive, date, and fig are also abundant.

There are several wildlife reserves in Israel, which are mainly inhabited by water birds and smaller animals. These include parts of the region of Arava in the south, Mount Carmel, Mount Meron, and the Hula Lake and marshes in the north. Pelicans, herons, partridges, and varieties of desert and mountain birds are some of the estimated 360 species found there.

Wildcats, gazelles, mongooses, jackals, foxes, weasels, wild boars, hares, badgers, and hyenas live in the Jordan river valley and near the Dead Sea. Snakes and lizards are found in the Negev Desert and other areas with desert-like conditions.

CITIES

Approximately 90 percent of Israel's 6,100,000 inhabitants live in some cities and towns. The three largest cities are Jerusalem (with 633,000 people), Tel Aviv-Yafo (with 348,000 people), and Haifa (with 265,000 people). A smaller but growing city in the south is Beersheba (with 163,000 people). Other urban centers include Netanya, Elat, Hebron, Rehovot, Ashdod, and Shechem.

JERUSALEM

Jerusalem is the capital of the Jewish state, although most foreign governments maintain their embassies in Tel Aviv. Like many cities whose past spans the ages, Jerusalem is an interesting and exciting mixture of old and new.

One very interesting feature of this ancient city is that it is a holy city for three distinct religions. In addition to its importance for the Jews, it holds great significance for Christians and Muslims. It has been the historical, spiritual, and national center of the Jewish people since King David proclaimed it the capital of the land in 1000 B.C. For Christians, it is the site of Jesus' crucifixion, burial, and resurrection. For Muslims it is the site of El-Aqsa Mosque, Islam's third holiest shrine.

For much of modern history, Jerusalem has been divided into two parts, the Jordanian and Israeli sectors. After 1967 the whole city came under Israel's control. Today there is the Old City and the New City.

THE OLD CITY The Old City, which is in the eastern part of Jerusalem, has been sieged by numerous wars since ancient times. The Six-Day War of 1967 reunited the two parts of Jerusalem (which was divided by the 1948 war) under Israeli rule.

Seven gates provide entrance to the ancient walled city. Modern Jerusalem is located west of the Old City and contains the modern commercial, residential, and industrial development.

There are five sections within the Old City: the revived Jewish Quarter, with its fragmented historical remains, was destroyed and rebuilt many times; the Christian Quarter, with its Holy Sepulchre; the Armenian Quarter, a residential area with ancient buildings, churches, and chapels; the densely populated Muslim Quarter, containing the ancient temple area; and the Temple Mount, the location of the Western Wall and the eight-sided Dome of the Rock, where Muslims believe the Prophet Muhammad ascended to heaven.

The Temple Mount, with its importance to Jews and Muslims alike, remains one of Jerusalem's most troublesome spots. The Old City has been declared "a protected cultural monument" by UNESCO.

Mea Shearim, a suburb of Jerusalem, is an example of a 'shtetel', or small town, which existed before the Holocaust in Eastern European Jewish communities.

Jerusalem at night.

THE NEW CITY The New City itself is not as spectacular as the Old City, and the name is misleading because parts of it are quite old. It has many areas that have great religious significance, such as the Garden of Gethsemane where Jesus prayed before he was arrested and crucified, the Mount of Olives and its ancient Jewish cemetery, and Mount Zion and King David's tomb. It also has office towers, high-rises, wide streets, and lovely parks.

Jerusalem, the capital of Israel, is the focal point of the Jewish people's national and spiritual life. It is the seat of the parliament, or Knesset (kuh-NESS-et), and home to the Hebrew University. The National Museum and important government and commercial institutions are also located here. The core of the city is commercial and residential, and its limited industrial areas are on the outskirts.

Jerusalem has two very distinct features. All of its older buildings are made of Jerusalem stone, which gives the city a uniform look. Also, it has a special fragrance, known as Jerusalem perfume, that is actually the scent of wild flowers that wafts through the air in the evening. This lovely aroma disappears when it is burned off with the morning sun.

TEL AVIV-JAFFA

Tel Aviv, which means hill of spring, was founded by a group of European immigrants living in the town of Jaffa, a neighboring seaport, almost a century ago. Jaffa grew rapidly within a short time and is characteristic of the fast pace that still exists there today. Tel Aviv united with Jaffa to become one city more than 50 years ago. Because of the melding of the two cities, the Tel Aviv-Jaffa area is also an interesting combination of old and new.

Tel Aviv, with Dizengof Square in the center.

Tel Aviv is the most cosmopolitan of Israel's cities. It is home to many foreign embassies and boasts numerous theater groups and museums. There are beautiful white beaches that hug the blue waters of the Mediterranean Sea. As a modern metropolis, however, Tel Aviv also suffers the problems of other big cities, including traffic jams, urban poverty, and development problems.

Jaffa, on the other hand, is one of the world's oldest cities. Its name is said to be derived from Japeth, son of Noah, who built the town. Jaffa has the legendary port from which the prophet Jonah set sail before being consumed by a great fish. In Jaffa today there are open markets and old forts that were built in the 10th century B.C.

Jaffa retains its Eastern character, perhaps because thousands of Israel's North African and Asian Jews reside here. The narrow alleys and streets are home to many artists, and among their stalls are outdoor cafés and beautiful antique shops. The port, said to be one of the oldest in the world, served as an entry point to thousands of Jews who came to start a new life. Its harbor is now closed to commercial shipping and has given way to Haifa as the new economic port.

HAIFA

Haifa has existed since the third century, but its main period of growth did not occur until the 20th century. The establishment of the Haifa-Damascus Railway led to development of Haifa's harbor by the British in 1929. It remains Israel's major Mediterranean port.

Israel's heavy-industry center is also in the Haifa area. Petroleum refineries, automobile and tire manufacturers, glass factories, cement works, steel mills, fertilizer producers, and shipbuilders are all located here.

Despite its prosperous industrial focus, Haifa is a splendid city whose beauty has been compared to that of San Francisco. It is also the world center for the Baha'i faith.

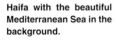

Haifa with the beautiful Mediterranean Sea in the background.

ISRAEL AND THE PALESTINIAN TERRITORIES

In 1967 Israel went to war with Egypt, Jordan, and Syria and won within six days (the war is now referred to as the Six-Day War). Israel gained land in the Golan Heights, the West Bank, the Gaza Strip, East Jerusalem, and the Sinai Desert.

Many Jewish immigrants flooded into Israel in the 1940s while many Palestinians left. Some Palestinians who did not leave formed the Palestine Liberation Organization (PLO) in 1964, which focused on freeing the land captured by Israel. During this time Israel signed a peace accord with Egypt and gave back the land gained in the Sinai Desert.

In 1987 the PLO launched the first intifada, an ongoing revolt, that began in the West Bank and the Gaza Strip and once again brought the topic of a Palestinian homeland back to the world's attention. In 1991 PLO leader Yasser Arafat and Israeli Prime Minister Yitzhak Rabin met in the United States and agreed to work on peace. Part of the Gaza Strip and the West Bank were given to Palestinian self-rule.

Despite Israel's withdrawal in 2000 from the security zone in southern Lebanon, failed peace talks in 2001 set off the second intifada. In 2002 Palestinians used suicide bombers and snipers to kill Israeli civilians in public places such as restaurants, markets, and public transportation. Israel's military entered many cities in the West Bank and the Gaza Strip to kill militants and destroy their infrastructure.

The disputed territories in Israel are the West Bank, the Golan Heights, and the Gaza Strip.

The West Bank is bounded by Israel on three sides and by the Dead Sea and the Jordan river to the east. It covers 2,270 square miles (15,231 square km). It includes what was formerly the Jordanian section of Jerusalem. In 1988 King Hussein of Jordan gave up claims to the West Bank so that the Palestinians there could establish an independent state.

Golan Heights is located at the point where Israel meets Syria to the southeast of Lebanon. It is a mountainous region of approximately 600 square miles (4,026 square km). Israel won this area in the 1967 war and formally placed it under Israeli "law, jurisdiction, and administration" in 1981. This territory is mainly occupied by Druze Arabs.

The Gaza Strip is adjacent to the Sinai Desert. Gaza was occupied by Egypt after the ceasefire in the War of Independence in 1948 and by Israel during the Six-Day War in 1967. In 1994 Israel handed over much of the Gaza Strip and the West Bank town of Jericho to the Palestinians to govern.

HISTORY

THE HISTORY OF THE LAND OF ISRAEL is closely related to that of the Jewish people. It is a blending of national and religious traditions dating back thousands of years to the era of the biblical patriarchs Abraham, Isaac, and Jacob. The Bible serves as the principal historical source for ancient Israel, one of the most studied ancient civilizations.

Yet modern Israel was only founded in 1948. Because of its prime location at the crossroads of Europe, Africa, and Asia, Israel was always the target of conquerors. Israel contains historic and spiritual sites significant to Judaism, Christianity, and Islam.

Opposite: **Citadel and Tower of David in the Old City of Jerusalem.**

Left: **Crusader forts in the ruins of Caesarea, an ancient port on the Mediterranean coast.**

EARLY HISTORY

Israel's history begins around 1800 B.C. with the migration of a group of herdsmen, led by Abraham, eastward from Mesopotamia. Setting up tents and digging wells, they settled in Canaan (Palestine's former name). These early Israelites wandered around Canaan for about three generations, until a famine forced them to migrate once again.

Abraham's grandson Jacob (also known as Israel) relocated with his 12 sons and their families to Egypt. These families grew in numbers and formed 12 tribes, collectively known as the Israelites. They remained in the Nile delta region for several centuries, and the Egyptian pharaohs eventually enslaved them.

Around 1300 B.C., the prophet Moses led the Israelites out of Egypt and slavery. They crossed the Red Sea and wandered around the Sinai Peninsula between Palestine and Egypt. After weeks or months of travelling in the desert the Israelites arrived at Mount Sinai and made a covenant, or sacred agreement, to worship only one God and to follow His Laws, the Ten Commandments. During the next 40 years

Moses educated the Israelites and laid the foundation of the community.

Around 1250 B.C., the 12 tribes returned to Canaan under the guidance of Joshua, who succeeded Moses. They encountered the Philistines, who had recently been forced from their homeland of Crete, and the Canaanites, who did not want the Israelites to settle there. For the next 200 years, these three groups fought for Canaan.

The Canaanites, who proved to be the weakest group, were defeated by the Israelites around 1125 B.C. However the Philistines had a superior military organization and better weapons. In around 1050 B.C., they defeated the Israelites, causing the 12 tribes to unite for strength under one king. Under Saul, however, there was dissension that continued until his death. David succeeded Saul and was able to unite the armies to defeat the Philistines and take over Canaan.

The remains of the main gate and city walls of biblical Shechem.

David established Jerusalem as the capital of the kingdom of Israel and began building the city. Upon his death, his son Solomon became king and completed the city and the First Temple of Jerusalem in which the Israelites could worship God. However, after Solomon's death, the different tribes began feuding, and they split the kingdom into two parts—Israel, with its capital at Samaria in the north, was home to 10 tribes, and Judah, with its capital at Jerusalem in the south, was home to the remaining two tribes. Citizens of the southern portion became known as the Jewish people.

Over the next few centuries, the two Hebrew kingdoms fought each other while at the same time tried to fend off attacks from outsiders.

A bust of Roman Emperor Hadrian, who crushed the Jews by destroying Jerusalem and forbidding Jews from entering it.

UNDER FOREIGN RULE

In the early eighth century B.C., the Assyrians from the north attacked and conquered Israel, exiling some Jews and taking others as slaves. Around 597 B.C., the Babylonians under their king Nebuchadnezzar, came and conquered Judah and destroyed the temple in Jerusalem. Many Jews were exiled to the Babylonian empire.

The Jews were freed less than 50 years later when Cyrus the Great of Persia conquered the Babylonians. Cyrus allowed the Jews to return to their homeland and rebuild the temple. However, Israel remained under the control of the Persians for another two centuries.

In 332 B.C. the Persian empire collapsed after being attacked by Alexander the Great of Macedonia. Alexander allowed self-government and religious freedom for the Jews. Later, the Ptolemies of Egypt and the Seleucids of Syria succeeded Alexander for control of the region. Eventually, the Seleucids tried to impose their Greek religion on the Jews. But under the guidance of a warrior named Judah Maccabee, the Jews revolted. Although Judas died, the Jews reestablished their independence in 141 B.C. after prolonged fighting.

Less than a century later, however, the Romans occupied the Jewish state. The land became a part of the Roman empire in 63 B.C., when it was renamed Judea. Over the next century, the Jews clashed with the Roman rulers, for they wanted to maintain their own religion and independence. Spurred on by a group known as the Zealots, the Jews launched the Great Revolt against the Romans. In the process, the Romans destroyed Jerusalem and the

MASADA

The strong will of the Jewish people to retain their freedom and their land goes back to ancient times. In A.D. 70, after Jerusalem fell to the Romans, freedom fighters known as the Zealots took refuge in a fortress high up a mountain known as Masada. A Roman army of 15,000 came to fight this Jewish force of less than 1,000. But it took them almost two years to eventually break through Masada's protective wall.

Realizing that they were outnumbered and that, at the very best, a life of slavery was all that was in store for them, the Zealots committed suicide rather than be captured. Under the leadership of Eleazar Ben Jair, the remaining 960 Jews organized and executed a mass suicide to ensure a hollow Roman victory.

Masada underwent extensive archeological digs in the 1960s, although it was identified more than a century before by two American scientists. Bones unearthed at the site went through radiocarbon dating tests, which determined that the skeletons are probably those of the Jewish rebels who killed themselves rather than surrender to the Romans.

Second Temple in A.D. 70, leaving all but the Western Wall in ruins.

In A.D. 132, Simon Bar Kokhba led Jewish fighters against the Roman empire for about three years before being crushed. To ensure that the Jews would not rise again, the Roman emperor Hadrian built a Roman city on the site of Jerusalem and called it Aelia Capitolina. He built a temple to the Roman god Jupiter on the site of the Temple of Jerusalem. The Romans did not allow the Jews to enter the city, and deported the Jews to colonies around the world.

This scattering, known as the Diaspora, sent most of the Jews to the shores of the Black Sea, the Greek Islands, and the coasts of the Mediterranean Sea. Some Jews fled to northern Europe and areas eastward. Regardless of where they settled, the Jews clung to their religious and cultural roots, one day hoping to return to their land.

THE FIGHT FOR PALESTINE

Palestine remained under Roman rule for the next 500 years. During that time, Christianity gained importance, as followers of Jesus of Nazareth spread his gospel.

After the fall of the western Roman empire in A.D. 476, the eastern Roman empire, or Byzantine empire, took over. These rulers did not take the rise of Islam seriously and underestimated the Arab military. In 638 the Arabs attacked and conquered Jerusalem. For the next 460 years, the country remained under Islamic rule. Some exiled Jews returned to Palestine during this time.

The early years of Arab rule were acceptable to the Jews, but later, the Muslim spiritual rulers introduced restrictions such as heavy taxes on non-Muslims. At this time, because of Jerusalem's importance to Christianity, soldiers from Europe launched a crusade to take the land back from Muslim rule. In 1099 the Crusaders conquered Jerusalem and ruled most of Palestine for 88 years.

In 1187 a Muslim army under Saladin recaptured Jerusalem. After Saladin's death, the Christians regained Jerusalem, but only until 1291, when the Egyptian Mamluks returned Muslim rule to Palestine for the next 225 years.

During this time, increasing numbers of Jews returned to the Holy Land. By 1517 the Mamluks had been overthrown by the Ottoman Empire. The Ottomans removed all Mamluk administrators, divided Palestine into districts, and allowed the Jewish community to expand. At this time, the vast majority of the population was of Arabic lineage and was spread out over Palestine. In contrast, the Jewish community centered around the more fertile and urbanized areas of Palestine.

Over the next 300 years, Jewish colonies grew, and Jews from Europe and the Orient migrated to Palestine. By the end of the 19th century, the dream of reestablishing a homeland had begun to take shape.

Above: **Tourists at a Crusader fortress in the ruins of Caesarea by the Mediterranean Sea.**

Opposite: **Ballista balls at the Apollonia-Arsuf Crusader city and fortress. The balls were used against the Mamluks, who attacked the city in 1265.**

Chaim Weizmann, the first president of Israel, meeting British Foreign Secretary Arthur Balfour (standing).

ESTABLISHING A HOMELAND

Several historical events helped establish the Israeli homeland. The movement to create a Jewish state became known as Zionism. In 1878 Jews purchased farmland in Palestine to set up a community. The first modern Jewish village was thus established. Around that time, there was much oppression of, and violence against, Jews in Eastern Europe. Four years later, an organized group of Jews fleeing Europe emigrated to Palestine. This immigration was called the First Aliyah.

In 1896, Theodor Herzl wrote *The Jewish State*, a book in which he suggested that Jews return to Palestine from countries where they were persecuted. One year later, the World Zionist Organization was established. Herzl's efforts inspired the Second Aliyah in 1904. Waves of immigrants entered Palestine after that and formed agricultural settlements throughout the country.

During World War I, British Foreign Secretary Arthur Balfour declared that his government favored "the establishment in Palestine of a national home for the Jewish people." Shortly after, British forces defeated the Ottoman empire and captured Palestine.

By this time, the Arabs also wanted independence. They saw the fall of the Ottoman empire as the opportunity for them to claim Palestine as their own, regardless of what the British government proposed. Despite the promise that the civil and religious rights of Arabs and Jews would be safeguarded, the roots of conflict were established. The British would rule over Palestine until 1948.

Between 1919 and 1933, the number of Jews in Palestine more than tripled to 200,000. As more Jewish oppression and persecution took place in Europe, Arab aggression against Palestinian Jews also increased, and

The ship *Jewish State* transported passengers to Israel illegally.

they revolted against British control. By 1937 the British realized that dividing the land was the best solution, but they limited the number of Jews that could emigrate to Israel and proposed the start of Arab and Jewish states within 10 years.

The crimes against Jews in World War II—six million European Jews were killed by the Nazis in the Holocaust—produced worldwide sympathy and support for the Zionist movement. Although the immigration limit remained in effect, some European Jews with nowhere to go entered Palestine. By 1946, the Jewish community had grown to nearly 500,000.

After the war, the question of Palestine came up again. Since they could satisfy neither side, the British placed the issue of dividing the land with the United Nations before leaving the region. The United Nations voted in favor of Palestine being divided into separate Arab and Jewish states, with Jerusalem having special international status. The Arabs rejected the plan. On May 14, 1948, Israel declared itself an independent state.

THE WAR YEARS

Within 24 hours of the British leaving the land, the combined forces of Lebanon, Jordan, Egypt, Syria and Iraq attacked Israel. The Israeli defense troops fought with weapons obtained through arms deals with Europe, and with the help of generous donations from foreign nations and individuals. After several months of fighting, a peace treaty was signed in January 1949. Israel had gained 50 percent more land than it had been given, as well as half of Jerusalem. The Arab nations, meanwhile, imposed an economic boycott on Israel.

The first Israeli elections were held after the ceasefire, with Chaim Weizmann elected president and David Ben-Gurion prime minister. The new government was admitted into the United Nations in May 1949.

Israeli tanks approach the Golan Heights during the Yom Kippur War.

An Israeli soldier carries a wounded comrade to safety during the period of heaviest fighting at the Golan Heights.

Clashes with Syria at the border started in the 1960s. When Israel threatened to fight back, Syria enlisted the help of Egypt. On June 5, 1967, Israel simultaneously attacked Egypt, Syria, and Jordan. It took only six days for the Israeli army to totally defeat its enemies. After the ceasefire, Israel had increased its land size by nearly 200 percent, conquering the Golan Heights, the Sinai Peninsula, and the West Bank of the Jordan River, plus all of Jerusalem. After the war, the Palestine Liberation Organization (PLO) stepped up its attacks on Israel and Jews. These attacks included hijacking airplanes and killing Israeli athletes at the 1972 Olympics in Germany.

Israel's insistence on keeping all of Jerusalem and retaining the recently acquired occupied territories caused another war. In October 1973, Syrian and Egyptian armies attacked Israel on Yom Kippur. Taken by surprise, Israel suffered losses but managed to beat back the attack. Sporadic clashes continued, and in 1975 an interim agreement was signed to bring about Israel's withdrawal from the Sinai and a United Nations peacekeeping force between Israel and Egypt.

From foes to friends: Israeli Prime Minister Menachem Begin (left) and President Anwar el-Sadat of Egypt.

ISRAEL TODAY

A breakthrough in the peace process came in 1977 when Egyptian President Anwar el-Sadat stated his willingness to meet with Israeli leaders to settle the Palestine issue. In 1978 United States President Jimmy Carter held a meeting with Sadat and Israeli Prime Minister Menachem Begin that resulted in a peace treaty. It spelled out Israel's complete withdrawal from the Sinai Peninsula in three years and eventual Arab self-rule in the West Bank and the Gaza Strip.

Though these were strong signs of progress toward peace in the Middle East, Lebanon, to Israel's north, was involved in a civil war. In addition, the border with Lebanon had been a source of trouble since a branch of the PLO took control of a portion of southern Lebanon. In 1982 ongoing clashes and an assassination attempt on an Israeli ambassador pushed Israel to invade Lebanon in order to attack the PLO. The Israeli army successfully drove out the PLO and helped create a political system led by the Lebanese Maronite Christians, who signed a peace treaty. However, under pressure from Syria, Lebanon canceled the agreement. After strong

Israeli Foreign Minister Shimon Peres signing the agreement in Washington on September 13, 1993, giving the Palestinians the right to self-rule in the Gaza Strip and the West Bank town of Jericho. Directly behind him are U.S. President Bill Clinton and PLO Chairman Yasser Arafat.

public opposition, Israel eventually withdrew its forces in 1985.

Two years later, Palestinians in Gaza rioted, causing general civil disobedience and unrest (known as an intifada) throughout Israel's occupied territories. A year later, the PLO declared itself an independent state. The PLO also recognized Israel's right to exist, a condition required by the United States before it would acknowledge the PLO. This move prompted the United States to start low-level peace talks between Israel and the PLO.

In 1991, during the Gulf War, Israel was attacked by Iraq. Although many missiles were fired at Israel, there were few casualties and only slight damage to buildings. Israel did not retaliate, but instead let a combined force from other countries defeat a world enemy.

In September 1993, Israel and the PLO signed a peace accord in which Israel would grant the Palestinians self-government in the Gaza Strip and the West Bank town of Jericho. This agreement was honored in May 1994, when Israel withdrew from Jericho and Gaza. However, further peace talks in 2001 failed, starting a second intifada. This led to further violent incidents involving Palestinian suicide bombers and snipers and the Israeli military.

GOVERNMENT

ISRAEL IS A PARLIAMENTARY DEMOCRACY with a unicameral (one-house) legislature, or parliament. This legislature—known as the Knesset—and the prime minister and the cabinet are responsible for governing Israel.

The president is the head of state, elected by the parliament to a five-year term. The president's role is mainly ceremonial, similar to that of the reigning monarch of the United Kingdom. Israel's president has little political power, except to grant pardons and appoint judges to the Supreme Court.

The president also appoints ambassadors and the state comptroller, who oversees budgets and the functions of all public bodies, and performs moral and educational functions. All residents of Israel are eligible to be presidential candidates.

Opposite: **A statue of the menorah, the traditional symbol of Judaism and the Knesset.**

Left: **David Ben-Gurion, Israel's first prime minister, making the Declaration of Independence speech in 1949.**

The Knesset building in Jerusalem.

THE KNESSET

The Knesset has 120 members who are elected for a maximum of four years; the 120 seats are given in direct ratio to the popular vote. Voters do not elect individuals, but political parties and subsequently the candidates they support. The more votes a party gets, the more seats it wins in the parliament.

No party has ever achieved a clear majority in the history of Israeli politics. The system is often criticized because voters have little control over the individuals who obtain these critical seats. However, those who support the system point out that it forces people to vote on issues rather than people.

The Knesset conducts business in a way similar to the British House of Commons, and its voting system is like the ones used in France and Germany. It has unlimited legislative authority, and enactments cannot be vetoed by the prime minister, president, or Supreme Court. The Knesset holds two sessions each year. The winter sessions opens after the High Holy Days, and the summer session opens after Independence Day.

BASIC LAWS

The Jewish state has no formal constitution, only a set of basic laws that were enacted with the intention that they would eventually become part of a constitution.

In the early years of statehood, Israeli lawmakers tried to compose a formal document. However, no agreement could be reached. So in 1950 the Knesset decided to gradually acquire a constitution, with the resolution stating that it would grow "chapter by chapter in such a way that each chapter will by itself constitute a fundamental law."

By the late 1980s, there were nine basic laws. These involve areas such as the function of the Knesset, the definition of Israel's borders, the role of the president, the operation of the government, the state economy, the army, the judiciary, elections, and Jerusalem.

There is no procedure to change the laws, although the Knesset can start a new government by simply getting a majority vote. But this is not likely to happen because the government is devoted to a rich tradition of democracy and the exchange of political ideas.

Israel's modern police force has 25,000 officers spread over 80 stations.

THE JUDICIAL SYSTEM

The judicial structure is composed of three courts: military, civil, and religious. Crime is handled by the civil court; marriage and divorce are administered by the religious court; and military matters are overseen by the military court.

Before taking office, judges must pledge allegiance to the state of Israel and take an oath to be neutral and just at all times. In addition, all judges, except those in the religious court, must vow loyalty to the laws of the state.

Israeli laws are borrowed from many areas, including Ottoman and British laws. Special investigative panels have been formed for unusual cases or situations.

The Supreme Court hears appeals from civil and criminal cases. It also hears cases that do not fall directly under the authority of the other courts. The number of justices that make up the Supreme Court is determined by the Knesset. In recent years, there have been 11 justices; a minimum of three must be present to hold a court session.

The Supreme Court is the principal guardian of fundamental rights in Israel and protects individuals from unfair or wrong practices by public agencies and officials. It has authority in almost all areas of Israeli life and functions almost like a formal constitution. Many Israelis consider the Supreme Court the guardian of democracy.

RELIGIOUS COURTS

Religious courts in Israel have authority over personal matters such as marriage, divorce, alimony, and religious wills of members of a religious community. Each major religious community has its own courts, deciding on all matters of their members' personal status and problems. If people of different religions are involved in a legal dispute, the president of the Supreme Court determines which court will have authority.

The seat of the Chief Rabbinate of Israel.

District courts can also have authority in personal legal matters if all parties involved agree on their participation.

Within the state of Israel, there are Jewish Rabbinical Courts, Muslim Courts, Christian Courts, and Druze Courts.

Tel Aviv City Hall.

THE CABINET

The cabinet, consisting of the prime minister and a number of other ministers, is Israel's central political power and the top policy-making body. The prime minister must be a member of the Knesset, but this is not required of the other cabinet ministers. The Knesset confirms the cabinet after the prime minister submits a list of names and a detailed report of the policies and fundamental principles of the cabinet.

The cabinet can be dissolved if the prime minister dies, if the Knesset officially reprimands it (known as "passing a censure"), or if it resigns as a group. Individuals can resign from the cabinet without disbanding it, but if the prime minister resigns, the whole cabinet must go with him or her.

Cabinet posts are divided among the various political parties or coalitions of the smaller ones, usually in proportion to the strength of the various parties.

ISRAEL'S MAJOR VOTING PARTIES

THE LABOR PARTY

This party's support has been based on the Histadrut (hiss-tahd-ROOT), the people of the *kibbutzim*, and the middle and upper-middle classes of European or Israeli origin.

THE LIKUD PARTY

This party consists mostly of Sephardic and Asian Jews. Sephardic Jews are from Aegean, Mediterranean, Balkan, and Middle Eastern countries. The Likud is considered to be a more conservative element of the Israeli political scene. It supports the importance of a free market economy for Israel.

THE RELIGIOUS PARTIES

The Sephardic Torah Guardians Association, Agudat Israel, and the National Religious Party combine to represent the Orthodox Jews. Their contributions are often seen as a crucial balance to the other parties.

LOCAL GOVERNMENT

Israel is divided into six administrative districts, each of which has a commissioner. Towns and cities with more than 20,000 people are run by municipal corporations, whereas smaller towns are run by local councils. Villages are collectively administered by regional councils.

There are 46 municipalities, 143 local councils, and 54 regional councils representing 700 villages, some of which are mainly Druze or Arab. All local government leaders are chosen through elections.

The local government provides basic services such as water supply, drainage, roads, parks, and social assistance, as well as sports, cultural, health, and educational facilities. To provide such services, the local government gets funds from a municipal tax, where the rates and budgets are authorized by the Ministry of the Interior.

ECONOMY

ISRAEL HAS HAD two distinct economic periods: the first from 1948 to 1972, and the second from 1973 to the present.

The beginning of the first period was extremely difficult. As a new state, Israel had a bare economic framework and limited natural resources and public services. In addition, Israel had to protect itself from Arab neighboring countries, which were not receptive to the establishment of the State of Israel, and at the same time accommodate new immigrants.

Israel faced no small task. It had to provide its new arrivals with food, housing and clothing, and set up civil service, monetary, and economic systems. In addition, the neighboring Arab countries had blocked free trade with Israel.

Left: **Buildings in the business district of Tel Aviv.**

Opposite: **A cement factory in Haifa. Cement manufacturing has been part of the Zionist dream ever since Theodor Herzl wrote about building a cement plant in *Altneuland* (Old New Land) in 1902.**

Above: **A chemical plant in Arad in the Negev Desert.**

Opposite: **Youth village where teenagers can learn about aircraft technology.**

ECONOMIC GROWTH

Israel overcame its early economic problems partly because of foreign investment and external aid. It received gifts, loans, and grants from the United States, donations from Jews around the world, and reparation funds from West Germany for crimes against Jews during World War II. That, combined with the resourcefulness of the Israelis, provided the great push for the country's economic growth. From the late 1940s until the mid-1970s, Israeli goods and services increased 10 percent annually, which was never matched by any other country in the free world for the same period.

The second economic period began in 1973. There were periods of strong growth followed by periods of stagnation and high unemployment. Nonetheless, in the 1970s, Israel had achieved a standard of living close to that of Western countries. The 1973 Yom Kippur War, however, created new economic woes. But the United States continued to provide aid, which further eased Israel's burden.

By 1990, Israel was producing goods and services worth $50 billion. Inflation was rampant, however, and strict price controls were imposed on essential goods. Tariffs were placed on imported goods, and a tax on travel was implemented. These efforts proved successful as inflation came down to a more manageable level.

Today, due to its limited natural resources, Israel continues to rely on imports. It still imports far more than it exports, creating a large trade deficit.

The government plays a significant role in Israel's economy; it owns and operates the postal, telegraph, and telephone systems as well as the railways. The government is also involved in public works.

Much of Israel's national income comes from manufacturing, agriculture, communications, computer-aided design, and medical electronics.

In 1996 exports of Israeli medical electronics equipment was worth $520 million. Israel's success in this field is due to the strong cooperation between its university researchers, hospitals, and industry. Medical equipment produced in Israel includes nuclear medical imaging, computerized tomography, magnetic resonance and ultrasound products.

Workers making bricks to be used in construction.

THE LABOR FORCE AND UNIONS

Nearly all workers in Israel are members of a union.

Although there are four labor unions, the most influential one is the Histadrut, or General Federation of Labor. It was created in 1923 by the Zionist workers' movement. The Histadrut also operates social service programs, develops industrial projects, and provides free education programs.

In 1989 the Histadrut had a membership of over one and a half million members. However, because of the privatization of the federation's healthcare system and its link to mandatory Histadrut membership, the number of members has fallen to around 700,000 with 100,000 young people belonging to the youth wing.

The Histadrut has no religious or ethnic criteria for its members. Arab and Druze workers are also full members. All types of workers make up the Histadrut: professional, technical, agricultural, civil service, and industrial.

The other three unions in Israel represent approximately 250,000 workers. Two of these, Poale I Agudat Israel (POH-ahl-leh ah-goo-DAHT ISS-rah-ell) and Ha-Poel Ha-Mizrachi (ah-poh-ELL ah-miz-rah-HEE), are religious unions that occasionally team up with the Histadrut on certain projects. Poale I Agudat Israel is a Jewish movement and political party that promotes adherence to religious law. It includes rabbinical, political, and executive branches and has a worldwide network of religious schools. The Ha-Poel Ha-Mizrachi combines the Torah, Zionism, and socialism into one movement. The fourth union is the National Labor Federation.

AGRICULTURE

Early settlers created the *kibbutzim* (collective farms) to fulfill their dreams in the "land of milk and honey." After 1948, however, when Arab nations blocked trade with the new Israeli nation, it became an economic necessity to develop other sources to produce food that previously had been imported from Arab countries.

Although only 20 percent of Israel's land could be farmed, the imagination and skills of the people paved the way for success. Marshland was drained and rocks moved to reveal usable farmland. Where there was no water, irrigation systems and greenhouses were built. All these increased the amount of arable land. Today nearly all of Israel's food needs are met by its agricultural production, and it even produces enough to be exported.

In spite of this, just five percent of Israel's labor force is engaged in agricultural activities.

Plastic farming, a new type of desert farming, is practiced near the Dead Sea.

Israelis test a NBC (Nuclear, Biological, and Chemical) Resistant Chamber at Beth El Industries. The chamber has air filters and can be used to protect people against biological and chemical warfare threats.

MANUFACTURING

Nearly one-third of Israel's workers are involved in manufacturing, and it is estimated that manufacturing generates nearly 30 percent of the national income.

The greatest concentration of heavy industry is in the Haifa area, while Tel Aviv is home to light industries such as textile manufacturing and food processing. Shoes, pencils, and printed items are produced in Jerusalem.

The electronics industry is providing a great boost to the Israeli economy, employing nearly 12 percent of the work force. Most of the electronic equipment manufactured is used domestically for defense or communications.

Another prospering sector is the diamond industry, although the gems are mined in other countries, such as Africa, Australia, Canada, and Russia. Diamond cutting, polishing, and trade originated in the town of Netanya in Israel. Today the center of these activities is Tel Aviv, where the Israel Diamond Exchange and Bourse is among the world's largest diamond markets.

MINERAL WEALTH

The Dead Sea provides large quantities of potash, bromine, and other salt deposits. The desert also yields valuable minerals: granite and phosphates in the Negev, and minerals for making glass and porcelain near Beersheba. Oil is found in the northern Negev and northeast of Beersheba.

FISHING

Fishing has developed into an important industry, although the Israelis must send boats as far out as the Ethiopian coast and the Atlantic Ocean to fish. This is because there are not a lot of fish along the Mediterranean and Red Sea coasts or in the Sea of Galilee. About one-third of the fish netted by Israeli fishing boats are freshwater varieties raised in artificial ponds, many of which are part of a *kibbutz*.

TOURISM

Tourism is a vital source of income and foreign currency for Israel, generating a total revenue of US$2.5 billion in 2001. The thriving industry brings in at least one million tourists to the country every year, 20 percent of whom are from the United States.

Israel's main tourist attractions are its historical sites and places of importance for three of the world's main religions. Devotees flock to the country during the seasons of Advent, Christmas, Ramadan, Hanukkah, Yom Kippur, Passover, Lent, and Easter.

As Israel is a country of immigrants, most Israelis maintain ties with family members and friends from all over the world. These visiting relatives and friends form a sizeable portion of tourist arrivals in Israel—31 percent in the year 2001.

However, Israel is also host to civil violence and warfare which break out frequently. Citizens, tourists, and religious pilgrims have been injured as a result of the violence. The volatile political and religious climate prevailing over Israel for the past few years has hurt the country's tourism industry.

There were about 2.7 million tourist arrivals in Israel in the year 2000, but this figure dipped

FOOD FROM THE DESERT

In the early 1900s, when the Zionist movement was starting, Jewish settlers encountered a poverty-stricken land of sand dunes and swamps. Their first order of business was to prepare the land for settlement and fully utilize whatever natural resources they could find.

This remains a priority for Israel. Right in the middle of the Negev Desert, where the temperature can exceed 120°F (49°C) and there is an annual rainfall of less than an inch, more than 250 agricultural settlements thrive. Israel has revolutionized its management of land and water resources in desert environments. What makes this feat so great is that the crops are not only irrigated using underground water, but also salt water!

This is possible through the process of desalination to remove salt from salt water. However, because desalination was very costly, the developers of the Negev settlement cultivated plants that did not soak up salt. It took scientists six years of experimentation to strike a correct balance of water nutrients, salt, and sun. The process, known as brackish-water agriculture, has made great strides. It has perfected the Negev tomato, which is quite popular in Europe because of its rich taste and ability to stay fresh for about a month. In addition, brackish-water agriculture has enabled Israel to export approximately 50 percent of its annual harvest.

The amount of cotton produced in Israel now surpasses that produced in Egypt and in the states of California and Arizona in the United States. Peanut production in Israel is more than four times that in the U.S. states of Georgia and West Virginia. It is hoped that in a few years the Negev will be the main producer of winter vegetables for Europe.

by 54 percent in 2001. This decrease translated to a loss of US$1.7 billion in revenues for the tourism industry in 2001. The stymied tourism industry has also affected the service industry, resulting in empty cabs and hotels and slower business at, or even closure of, restaurants.

The unstable local climate is aggravated by attacks on U.S. entities, namely the USS Cole destroyer in Yemen and the World Trade Center buildings in New York in the United States. A weakening of the U.S. dollar against European currencies further softened the U.S. tourist market to Israel.

Opposite: **A view of Golan Heights, which Israel conquered during the Six-Day War in 1967 with Egypt, Syria, and Jordan.**

ENVIRONMENT

ISRAEL'S DEDICATION TO environmental preservation can be traced to the Bible, which informs people of their rights and responsibilities as stewards of the earth. For example, the book of Genesis calls on people to "...rule over the fish of the sea and the birds of the air and over every living creature that moves on the ground..." (1:28), while Deuteronomy 20:19 instructs "...do not destroy [its] trees...".

Teachings on preserving the land through conservation and development are found throughout Jewish law and literature. For instance, there is a command in the Bible to let the land rest every seventh year, which is practiced throughout Israel, and which has been cited as a means of soil preservation and improvement.

The Israelis have taken a land lacking in water with a varied and difficult climate and increasing population density, and made it blossom. The people of this historically arid land have become world leaders in agricultural innovation, pollution prevention and control, and waste management.

Opposite: **Israelis enjoying the view of Mount Tabor and Jezreel Valley from the Mount of Precipitation.**

Left: **Dry land in the West Bank is cultivated through dry farming practices.**

This industrial factory at Haifa belches smoke as goats graze nearby.

AIR POLLUTION

With increased urbanization and industrialization, Israel has developed programs to deal with air pollution, water shortages, and increasing amounts of solid and hazardous waste.

The main sources of air pollution in Israel are energy production, vehicular traffic and industrial activities. Israel has worked to improve the air quality by establishing a nationwide framework for monitoring and analyzing air pollution, by implementing legislation and enforcement, and by initiating research and development to examine alternative energy resources.

The national air monitoring system that collects and analyzes data on air quality includes 24 sophisticated monitoring stations, three regional centers, and a national control center. This system monitors the air for pollutants such as ozone and sulphur dioxide. Israel is an international leader in the development and use of solar power and other alternative energy sources.

WATER CONSERVATION

Water shortage is a major environmental issue in Israel. This is due to a lack of natural water resources and a rising demand for water from a growing population. Contamination of natural water supplies is also a problem. In 2001 residents in parts of Israel were warned against drinking tap water as it was discolored and contaminated with ammonia. This contamination was due to seepage of fertilizer into three nearby wells.

To combat the water shortage, Israel has undertaken a multifaceted strategy that combines education, technical development, and financial incentives. Technological innovations have been pursued both to use water more efficiently and to treat and reuse waste water. Israel has been able to conserve water through the development of innovative irrigation methods and the introduction of crops that can live on limited water or on salt water. The government has built water treatment plants in the major cities and recycles 70 percent of its waste water for irrigation of non-food crops and animal consumption.

The water line at the Sea of Galilee has been gradually receding for years. This is due to overuse of the Jordan River, which flows from Lebanon to Israel, where it joins the Sea of Galilee and then the Dead Sea.

WASTE MANAGEMENT

Waste disposal in Israel was largely unregulated until 1993, when the government began developing central sanitary landfills and closing illegal dumpsites.

Israel generates 7.2 million tons of waste annually, and the government is working on plants which convert this waste to useful energy. Israelis, who produce an average of 2.2 kilograms of solid waste per person every day, are also encouraged to reduce waste by recycling more goods.

Israel manages hazardous substances with numerous strictly enforced laws and regulations; a national response system that can send inspectors to the scene of a hazardous substance accident within a half hour; a center for hazardous waste treatment and disposal; and a response-and-information system.

NATURE CONSERVATION

Aware of its relatively small size and limited natural resources, Israel has taken steps to conserve whatever flora and fauna it has.

About 25 percent of Israel's land is protected. The country has 155 nature reserves, which include the wide range of Israel's various landscapes from forests to deserts. In addition, several of Israel's plants and animals (such as the leopard, gazelle, ibex, and vulture) have been given protected status. To preserve the natural landscapes, Israel has established 41 national parks and implemented a national strategy for the development and conservation of forests.

A project at the Hai Bar reserves in Arava and on Mount Carmel involves reintroducing animal species that once roamed Israel into their former natural habitats. These species include the white oryx, ostrich, Persian fallow deer, roe deer, and Asiatic wild ass.

Wildflowers, which used to grow in abundance in Israel, had almost disappeared due to overpicking in the 1960s. A successful government campaign managed to repair this damage. Today, Israelis are careful to avoid picking wildflowers, which once again bloom in profusion throughout the country.

In October 2000, about 20,000 Israelis gathered around the Sea of Galilee and linked their hands to form a 'big hug'. This campaign was designed to promote awareness of the water shortage problem and round up efforts for water conservation in Israel.

ENVIRONMENTAL LEGISLATION

Over the last 10 years, Israel has worked to develop comprehensive environmental legislation. There are approximately 24 laws, which have criminal sanctions in the form of fines and imprisonment, and 56 regulations that deal with environmental issues.

Israel emphasizes strict enforcement of its environmental legislation through licensing and supervision as well as inspection and prosecution. Industries and businesses must fulfill certain conditions before they are licensed to operate. Parties who break the rules may have their businesses closed down.

Enforcement is done by the government through an investigating unit called The Environmental Patrol and through recruitment of volunteer civilians as Cleanliness Trustees who assist in the enforcement of the Maintenance of Cleanliness Law. This law ensures general cleanliness and order in Israel and prohibits such acts as littering and the improper disposal of waste, building debris, or vehicle scrap.

MAJOR ENVIRONMENTAL LAWS IN ISRAEL

Law	Focus	Year
Licensing of Business	Requires businesses to operate under a license, which is subject to approval by relevant ministries, including the Ministry of the Environment. This license is issued only if a business prevents hazards and nuisances, provides reasonable sanitary conditions, and obeys planning and building laws, among other things.	1968
Planning and Building	Regulates construction and land use. Establishes institutional framework for environmental planning. The National Outline Scheme under this provision lays down the planning structure of the whole of Israel and assigns purposes for various areas: industrial, recreational, nature reserves, and so on. Licenses are also required for building roads or erecting buildings to ensure that they conform to this plan.	1965
Water	Regulates water rights, water conservation, re-use of treated waste water, and prevention of water pollution in Israel. According to this law, all sources of water in Israel are public property, even if that body of water runs in or under an individual's land. All Israelis must use water efficiently and sparingly to prevent wastage. They also must not cause pollution by throwing any liquid, solid, or gaseous substances into a body of water or near it.	1959
Hazardous Substances	Provides the framework for the management of hazardous substances. The Ministry of the Environment uses this law to create regulations on the classification of poisons and toxic materials and on their use, packaging, storage, transfer, and maintenance.	1993

ISRAELIS

THE ESTIMATED POPULATION OF ISRAEL is six million. Of that figure, around 80 percent are Jewish and 20 percent non-Jewish, mostly Arabs.

World events have had an impact on the population statistics of Israel: the breakup of the Soviet Union resulted in more than 340,000 Jewish immigrants added to Israel's population between mid-1989 and the end of 1991; famine in Ethiopia in the mid-1980s resulted in an airlift of 10,000 Ethiopian Jews to Israel; and in the spring of 1991, Operation Solomon, an airlift of 14,500 additional Ethiopians, was carried out just before the Ethiopian government fell to rebel forces.

The Law of Return, which grants citizenship to any Jew who migrates to Israel, ensures that there will always be a place for Jews in Israel.

Opposite: **Arab Israeli Boy Scouts from Nazareth.**

Left: **People waiting for a bus in Jerusalem.**

Jewish flower vendors in Tel Aviv.

JEWISH ETHNIC GROUPS

The Diaspora—the dispersion of Jews dating back to the second century —was the most significant influence on the creation of different ethnic groups within Judaism. These Jews were scattered throughout the world and lacked a homeland. Although they clung to the study and observance of Jewish religious scriptures and attempted to follow the laws and rituals of the religion, they adopted many foreign attitudes in their new lands.

Indeed the Jews of Israel share a common identity through Judaism, but they are not an identical people. Coming to the Holy Land from more than 100 countries, they bring numerous languages and customs.

There are two dominant Jewish ethnic groups in Israel—the Ashkenazim and the Sephardim. The Ashkenazim, whose name comes from the old Hebrew word for Germany, are Jews from northern and eastern Europe and Russia. The Hebrew word *Sephard* means a Jewish person from Spain. In the 15th century, Jews who refused to convert to Christianity were forced to leave Spain and Portugal. Many fled to North Africa, Italy, and what is now Turkey. Today, Sephardic refers to Jews from Aegean, Mediterranean, Balkan, and Middle Eastern backgrounds.

The Ashkenazim were among the leaders of the Zionist movement who brought with them the Western lifestyles that set the pace for Israel's cultural and intellectual development. The Sephardim, on the other hand, made up the majority of immigrants after 1950. Many were from small villages in North Africa, Iraq, Syria, Greece, and Turkey.

An Israeli police officer.

Another major difference between these two groups was their view of Israel. The Sephardim saw life in Israel as delivery from exile and the fulfilment of a biblical prophecy. The Ashkenazim had suffered persecution in their former homelands and hoped to find political and religious freedom in the Jewish state.

Until recently, the Sephardim placed less emphasis on political matters than did the Ashkenazim, who remain Israel's more influential group. The Likud Party's 1977 electoral victory is closely aligned to the Sephardic Jews' somewhat recent involvement in politics, and it is seen as a positive step toward lessening the social and economic gaps between these two groups.

Above: **Children of Ethiopian immigrants with Israeli volunteer teachers.**

Opposite: **A fruit seller at a market in Tel Aviv.**

IMMIGRATION TRENDS

The word *aliyah*, which literally means going up, refers to the immigration of Jews to the land of Israel. Five major periods of *aliyah* have contributed to the development of Israel's people.

The First Aliyah, from 1882 to 1903, brought 25,000 Jews, mostly fleeing persecution in Russia. These Jews were partly influenced by Hibbat Tzion, or Love of Zion, a movement for the reestablishment of Israel, which started among the Jews in Russia and spread to other countries at the end of the 19th century. Their arrival in Palestine doubled the Jewish population and caused the first clash between the Ashkenazim and the Sephardim. These immigrants were less religious and more interested in establishing a Jewish nation, while the Palestinian Jews were not political but more religious. Several thousand Jews from Yemen also arrived with the First Aliyah.

The First Aliyah immigrants were responsible for starting early rural settlements. It was also during this time that Hebrew was revived as a means of communication, aided by the setting up of Hebrew schools.

The Second and Third Aliyot, from 1904 to 1923, brought 76,000 Jews mainly from Russia and Poland. These *aliyot* were encouraged by the Balfour Declaration and British occupation of Palestine, which later spurred the creation of the Jewish state of Israel. Immigrants of the Second and Third Aliyot created *kibbutzim*, cooperative villages called *moshavim*, the Histadrut labor federation, and the education system. They used Hebrew in all areas of Jewish life and laid the foundation for modern Tel Aviv.

Approximately 349,000 central European immigrants came in the Fourth and Fifth Aliyot, from 1924 to 1939. Many of them migrated to escape Nazism, which began when Adolf Hitler came to power. Immigrants of the Fourth and Fifth Aliyot, many of whom were professionals and businessmen, contributed greatly to the cultural and economic development of the country. These immigrants settled in the major cities and towns; half of them chose Tel Aviv, where they were able to continue a way of life that was similar to what they had grown accustomed to in Europe.

Immigrants from 1948 to 1969 numbered 1.25 million; half were from Asia and North Africa. Compared to the Askenazim, the Sephardim were socially and economically disadvantaged from the start of their stay in Israel. The Sephardim Jews lacked skills and education and had to accept lower paying jobs. They also often had larger families and lived in marginal neighborhoods, and this hampered their social mobility.

While in theory the Sephardim Jews were accepted into Israeli society, the rift between them and the Askenazim gained a strong foothold as problems of discrimination and inequality persisted.

Arab women shopping in a Beersheba market.

ISRAELI ARABS

The Israeli Arab population, more than three-quarters of whom are Sunni Muslims, has remained concentrated in the northern and Haifa districts since 1948. Israel's establishment in 1948 also absorbed one million Palestinians, who stayed on and became part of Israel.

Approximately two-thirds of Israel's Arab citizenry live in urban areas and are mainly employed in construction and industry rather than agricultural occupations. Arabs form 20 percent of Israel's population.

The standard of living for Arabs in Israel has improved since Israel's statehood. As citizens, the Arabs share in the health, welfare, and education systems. The infant death rates have declined since the end of the British mandate period.

The Arabs make up an ethnic and religious minority in the country. Arab citizens have voting rights and government representation, and are exempted from military service. They also have less access to land ownership and certain types of government funding than Jews.

Arab sympathy for the Palestine Liberation Organization also causes resentment and ill feelings between the Jewish majority and the Arab minority.

Israeli Arabs generally remain loyal to their cultural, religious, and political backgrounds. Like the Jews, even though they share a common ethnic identity, the Arabs are made up of different groups of people. This prevents them from uniting as a single pressure group that can have an effective impact on the Jewish majority.

THE BEDOUINS

The Bedouin population in Israel represents some 40 tribal groups living primarily in the Negev Desert in southern Israel. Traditionally they were nomads; however they are now settled in small villages and towns. It is difficult to determine the exact number of Bedouins, but reliable estimates put their number in Israel at 150,000.

Nomadic Bedouins eat, sleep, travel, and trade in much the same way that they did 1,500 years ago. Along with their camels, they are well-known for having conquered the desert. They live mostly off camel, goat, and sheepherding and are considered good traders. They are also great hosts; whenever they have visitors, they always give their very best food.

Bedouin nomads have an uncanny tracking ability; they are known as the best desert trackers in the world. They are able to find traces of people or animals in the sand, tell if the animal had been running, or whether a man or woman was carrying equipment.

This very special skill has made Bedouins very valuable to the Israeli army, especially for guarding the borders. They are among the few Israeli Arabs who can serve in the army, and are always called upon to track down enemy troops who have broken through Israel's border defenses.

An Israeli Bedouin.

The Bedouins pride themselves on their hospitality, which they treat their guests to, along with protection. A guest who dines in a Bedouin home has protection for as long as three days after the meal.

A Druze from the village of Boukata in the Golan Heights.

THE DRUZE

The Druze are an Arab sect that established its own branch of Islam in the 11th century. One of the most fascinating things about this group is that they have kept their religion a secret. They do not accept converts, leave their faith, or marry other than their fellow Druze. This exclusive sect lives by its own principles and prefers to remain closed to public scrutiny.

The Druze live in the area where Syria, Lebanon, and Israel meet. They number 99,000 in Israel, many living in the Golan Heights, and make their living by farming. The Israeli Druze have adapted to Israeli society better than any other Arab group and, unlike most Arabs, are pro-Israel. For years, the Druze have have served in the army, and they have representatives in the Knesset.

The one exception to this friendly Jewish-Druze relationship involves the Druze of the Golan Heights. Although these Arabs have been Israeli citizens since the 1967 war, they feel they are unwilling victims of the Israeli-Syrian dispute, and so they choose not to vote and are not drafted into the army. Unlike other Arabs in the Gaza Strip and the West Bank, however, they do not openly oppose Israel.

OTHER MINORITIES

There are also small communities of Karaites (30,000 people) in the towns of Ashdod, Beersheba, and Ramla; Circassians (3,000) in two villages in Galilee; and Samaritans (550) in the towns of Holon and Shechem.

THE TEN LOST TRIBES OF ISRAEL

A recent wave of Sephardic immigrants, the Ethiopian Jews, have quite different religious customs from the other Jewish groups that have returned to the Holy Land—so different that their "Jewishness" was a topic of conversation among Israel's chief rabbis. The differences are the result of the Ethiopians' isolation from mainstream Judaism.

What caused that isolation? According to Jewish history, 12 ancient tribes lived in Palestine. After years of fighting among themselves, the land was divided into the kingdom of Israel in the north, where 10 tribes lived, and the kingdom of Judah in the south, home to the remaining two tribes.

In 722 B.C. the kingdom of Israel was conquered by the Assyrians, and its inhabitants exiled to "Halah and Habor by the river Gozan, and in the cities of Medes." These 10 tribes were never seen again, and they are known as the Ten Lost Tribes of Israel.

Biblical prophets Isaiah, Jeremiah, and Ezekiel promised that the lost tribes would eventually be reunited with the rest of the nation, and this has kept the memory and search for the tribes alive. Thus many think that the return of the Ethiopian Jews to Israel is a 10 percent fulfillment of that prophecy.

Throughout history, attempts have been made to explain how the 10 tribes disappeared and to discover them. An 1871 book even presented 47 proofs that the British were part of the Ten Lost Tribes.

The search goes on. For the last three decades, an organization called Amishav has been dedicated to finding lost Jews from around the world. The group's mission is to return these people to the land, for according to biblical prophecy, the Messiah will come only after all 12 tribes return to Israel.

However, there are skeptics who dismiss the Ten Lost Tribes as nothing but legend, as there is no conclusive evidence to prove their existence.

LIFESTYLE

A FUNDAMENTAL PRINCIPLE of the state of Israel is that every Jew has the right to settle there. The Law of Return gives legal status to this principle; it grants automatic citizenship to any Jew who wants it. Also guaranteed is freedom of worship. As a result of this, there are many lifestyles within this tiny nation. The range of lifestyles among the Israelis does not fall along religious lines; the life of the Ultra-Orthodox Jew no more resembles the life of the secular Jew than it does the life of the nomadic Bedouin or the mysterious Druze.

Israeli society is a kaleidoscope of customs, traditions, and beliefs. The ways in which these numerous groups conduct their lives and interact with one another presents a very interesting picture.

Opposite: **Inside the Seven Stars Shopping Centre in Herzlia.**

Left: **Modern housing for the citizens of Jerusalem.**

Young Israelis play the Darbukah, a Middle Eastern hand drum.

THE JEWISH HOMELAND

The goal of Zionism was to establish a homeland where Jews would not be a minority. By attaining this independence, Jews would no longer be dependent on others for their safety and well-being. Also, the early pioneers felt that no matter where the Jews lived, they would be spiritual prisoners of a non-Jewish society—they would always question what the non-Jewish world might say about their every move.

Theodor Herzl, a German Jewish writer, started the Zionist movement in the late 1800s. He penned the book *Altneuland*, in which he proposed his vision of the Jewish state. This vision was realized about 50 years later when Israel declared its statehood in 1948. Zionist pioneers felt that making the Jewish people citizens of their own land would ease anti-Semitism and give Jews spiritual and emotional freedom.

JUDAISM IN EVERYDAY LIFE

Judaism is the unifying force and basis for the establishment of the state of Israel. The bond among Jews strengthens during times of Arab opposition. Nonetheless, a deep division exists among Jews and that continues to be an important issue.

The major difference among Israelis is between religious Jews and secular Jews, and over the separation of synagogue and government. It is estimated that more than 75 percent of Israel's Jewish population considers itself secular. While it would seem that the religious minority would not play a significant role in Israeli day-to-day life, quite the opposite is true. Religious groups form political parties, and even a small group can exert considerable political influence.

Religious Jews feel that because Israel is a Jewish state, it should be based on Jewish customs and laws, and that the secular part affecting Jewish life should be checked. They maintain that Jewish tradition is what held the Jewish people together during centuries of separation, and it is what led to the establishment of Israel.

An Orthodox Jew praying by the Wailing Wall.

On the other hand, secular Israelis insist that religious involvement should be a matter of personal choice and that in a democracy, separation of religion and government is important.

Furthermore, because Judaism is considered not just a religion but a way of life, secular Jews believe that the imposition of religious ritual and tradition prevents them from enjoying the religious freedom that is guaranteed in Israel.

A *kibbutznik* mixes feed for fish in a cement mixer.

LIFE ON THE KIBBUTZ

The *kibbutz* is one of the original contributions of the Jewish settlers in modern Israel. A *kibbutz* is a community where people live and work together, growing their own food and sharing everything. All members are equal.

The first *kibbutz* was formed in 1909, when seven pioneers working near the Sea of Galilee asked the Jewish National Fund to allow them to farm a piece of land. These early settlers felt that working the land would bind the Jews to their new homeland. Kibbutz Degania was the result of this idea, and the *kibbutz* has been a working institution for more than 80 years.

Today, there are more than 800 *kibbutzim* (the plural of *kibbutz)*, ranging in size from 100 members to as many as 2,000. Land is leased to the *kibbutznik* (residents of the *kibbutz*) for a 49-year period, at the end of which the lease can be renewed. Kibbutz Degania is one of the most successful settlements in Israel. It is so large that it had to be divided into two: Degania Alef (A) and Degania Bet (B).

The *kibbutz* provides for all the needs of its residents, and no one is paid for his or her work. Many *kibbutznik* eat in communal dining rooms, and get their clothing from the community's shop and have it washed at a communal laundry or repaired at a communal tailor shop. All cars and trucks on the *kibbutz* are owned by the community.

Each *kibbutz* strives to be fair to every member. Decisions are made at weekly meetings, and everything that is produced and earned is shared equally with all members. Committees are elected to deal with certain management issues.

There is one aspect of family life that really sets *kibbutznik* apart. In many villages, children live separately from their parents in houses with other children of their age group. In the evenings, they spend time with their fathers and mothers in the parents' living quarters. In other *kibbutzim*, however, residents feel that family life is central to Jewish culture, and the family lives together in private *kibbutz* housing. All *kibbutz* youngsters, however, have their own jobs and responsibilities and often have to take care of crops. They attend schools that are independent of the Israeli school system, where the schedule includes certain hours on the farm and teachers labor with students in maintaining the land.

While farming is still very important on the *kibbutz*, many *kibbutzim* engage in other industries such as textiles, furniture production, and even telecommunications equipment production. Economic realities have caused many *kibbutzim* to consider nontraditional methods of making a profit for survival. Some have opened day-care centers for children from neighboring towns or have begun charging outsiders admission for the use of the *kibbutz* swimming pool. Some have even hired non-*kibbutznik* managers to keep the operations profitable.

There are also a number of religious *kibbutzim* that choose the traditional principles of labor, equality, and communal living, but combine them with an organized way of life according to Judaism. Dealing with daily chores of the farm on the sabbath has required the religious *kibbutznik* to come up with creative solutions, such as automatically regulated milking equipment.

Although only 4 percent of Israelis live on the *kibbutzim*, *kibbutz* life is considered admirable, and *kibbutznik* are treated with great respect. They make up about 14 percent of army officers, and many serve in the Knesset.

Arab children going to school in the Old City section of Jerusalem.

EDUCATION

Israeli law states that for Jews, primary education should focus on "the values of Jewish culture and the achievements of science; on love of the homeland and devotion to the state and the Jewish people; on training in agricultural work and handicraft; on fulfillment of pioneering principles; and on the aspiration to a society built on freedom, equality, tolerance, mutual assistance, and love of mankind."

Free education is a cornerstone of democracy in the state of Israel, and it is a prime national concern. Approximately 8 percent of the annual budget is devoted to education. In Israel, education is compulsory and free for children (Jews and Arabs alike) between the ages of five and 16. The system includes kindergarten (the purpose is to ensure that all students know Hebrew), six-year primary schools, three-year junior high schools, and three-year high schools. After high school, students take an exam to determine if they can go on to college. University education is usually pursued after military service.

The government runs three types of schools: secular (without religious connections), religious (which devote attention to religious laws, prayers, and the Talmud, a supreme sourcebook of law), and schools for Israeli Arabs. Private religious schools, run by independent orthodox organizations, are also available. In religious institutions, boys and girls are educated in separate classes. After graduating from these schools at the age of 14, boys generally enter a *yeshiva* (yeh-SHI-vah), or religious college, to become rabbis.

Students attend school six days a week. In primary school, they study Hebrew, the Bible, geography, science, mathematics, crafts, art and music, history, and physical education. English classes start in the fifth grade, and Arabic is often taught as a third language.

An Israeli teacher with her class.

Children from Arab villages and Bedouin camps can go to school too. For the Bedouins, there are field schools that move with the population. Arabic is the language of instruction in all Israeli Arab schools, and Hebrew is taught as a second language. Most teachers in these schools are Arabs, and emphasis is placed on Arabic history and culture. Textbooks used are direct Arabic translations of the Hebrew texts used in Jewish schools. In the Gaza Strip and the West Bank, schools are under the authority of the local municipality.

Post-secondary education is open to anyone who is qualified. There are 12 institutes of higher education in Israel. The Hebrew University and the Tel Aviv University educate approximately 40,000 students between them. Others include the Ben Gurion University, Haifa University, and Bar Ilan University. The Technion in Haifa and the Weizmann Institute in Rehovot are well-known technology and science schools.

Young Israeli soldiers taking a rest on the sidewalk.

THE ARMY

The Israeli army (also known as the Israel Defense Forces, or IDF) plays an important part in the lives of all young Jewish Israelis. The average Sabra grows up knowing that once he or she reaches the age of 17 or 18, military service is next.

All Jewish citizens must serve, except those who are handicapped or extremely religious. Although military service is compulsory, Israelis look upon it with pride and joy. Men serve for three years, women for two. In addition, men must serve four weeks in the active reserves each year until they reach the age of 51. Unmarried women remain in the reserves until they are 34.

The military also serves a social function in Israel. Because Jews who migrate to Israel are granted immediate citizenship, the new arrival's first duty is military service. While in the army, he or she learns to speak and read Hebrew, studies the history and geography of the new country, and is taught everything about Israeli citizenship.

While in the army, many get a head start on a career by seeking army jobs in fields that they would like to enter later on. Becoming an officer is also beneficial; the most successful executives, managers, and government employees were officers during their military service, so the youth generally take their time in the IDF very seriously.

ULPAN

The *ulpan* (ool-PAHN) teaches immigrants about the cultures of Israel and offers intensive Hebrew language lessons. These lessons help immigrants to better assimilate into their new environment. New immigrants may also receive the absorption basket, a form of financial aid.

There are several types of *ulpan*: for example, the residential *ulpan* is popular among professionals and meets for five hours a day for five months; the *kibbutz* for younger people has students working for four hours and studying the rest of the day.

YOUTH MOVEMENTS

Israeli youth organizations are active as extracurricular education and recreation for children and teenagers between the ages of 10 and 16. Almost every young Israeli is a member of a youth movement. The largest group has ties with the Histadrut labor organization, serving as a type of junior trade union that provides vocational education and union benefits.

The Israel Scout Federation meets weekly for games, cultural activities, and educational programs. Members wear khaki uniforms and colorful kerchiefs, and leaders stress the pioneering spirit and the benefits of living off the land. This group is associated with the International Scouting Movement. Bene Akiva is the largest religious youth movement.

A Circassian father and his children.

THE FAMILY

The family has always been important in Jewish life. Although many different ethnic groups, lifestyles, and attitudes make up the Israeli population, one thing that remains the same is the importance of the close-knit family unit.

For most Israeli families, regardless of whether they are secular or religious, *kibbutznik* or city-dweller, dinner time is usually the focal point of the family experience, for it is often the only time other than on the sabbath that the entire family can be together.

Because of the religious atmosphere in Israel, most families celebrate the Jewish festivals as holidays, and they cherish this time as quality time with the family.

MARRIAGE

In Judaism, marriage is considered the ideal state of existence; it is the basic social institution that God established at the time of creation. For Jews the purpose of marriage is companionship, self-fulfilment, and procreation.

The marriage ceremony consists of two acts: *kiddushin* (ki-DOO-shin) and *nisuin* (ni-SOO-in). *Kiddushin* is the legal "receiving" of the bride by the groom. The groom hands over an object of value—usually a ring— to the bride in the presence of two witnesses and says, "Behold, you are consecrated unto me with this ring, according to the law of Moses and Israel." By this act, he states his intention to reserve the bride for himself. By accepting the item of value, the bride indicates that she agrees.

In the *nisuin* ceremony, the mothers of the bride and groom lead the bride to the *huppah* (koo-PAH), or bridal canopy, which symbolizes the groom's house, and the mothers give the bride their blessings. The groom is accompanied to the *huppah* by the fathers of the bride and groom. The ceremony is customarily performed in the presence of a *minyan* (MIN-yahn), a group of 10 men. After the bride and groom drink from a goblet of wine, the groom places the wedding ring on the index finger of the bride's right hand and repeats what he said during the *kiddushin*. Seven marriage blessings are recited over another goblet of wine by several different people, and the groom concludes the ceremony by crushing a glass under his right foot. (The breaking of glass signifies the mourning of the destruction of the temple in Jerusalem in A.D. 70.) After the ceremony, the couple is led to a private room in which they spend time together. It is only after this private time that they are considered husband and wife.

A bride and groom pose for pictures.

DIVORCE

In Judaism, when a married couple no longer shares a loving relationship, it is acceptable to get a divorce. Marriage and divorce are seen as acts of free will. Divorce, nevertheless, saddens and deeply hurts all who are involved.

In Israel, Jewish divorce cases go through the Jewish Rabbinical Court. The *get* (geht) is the bill of divorce, the document releasing the woman from her marriage. The *get* itself is written on heavy white paper. Special ink that cannot be erased is used to write the text so that no changes can be made after it is written.

According to Jewish law, only after the *get* is delivered into the hands of the wife does the divorce take place.

At the ceremony, the husband and wife meet before the

These Israeli babies are dressed up for Palm Sunday, the Sunday before Easter.

beth din (beht-DIN), or Rabbinical Court, and the husband hands the wife the 12-line *get*. Until she holds the document, the divorce is not finalized. After receiving the piece of paper, the wife either takes a few symbolic steps or walks into another room. At that point, she is considered once again an unmarried woman.

BIRTH RITUALS

Historically, there is greater joy at the birth of a boy than of a girl. Jewish birth rituals differ for boys and girls.

Jewish boys are initiated into Judaism on the eighth day of life, the day of the *brit* (brit), or ritual circumcision. The *brit* is a symbol of a boy's joining the community of Israel. A *mohel* (maw-HELL), who is a ritual circumciser, performs the ceremony, which generally takes place

BAR MITZVAH

At age 13 Jewish males celebrate their Bar Mitzvah, which literally means 'son of commandment' (Bat Mitzvah or 'daughter of commandment' for girls). It is from this point on that Jewish youths are obligated by religious duties, such as fasting on Yom Kippur, among other things. They also have the right to participate in religious services, and be counted as one of the 10 people, or *minyan*, whose presence are needed to form a congregation for communal prayer and to perform parts of certain religious services.

A child attends religious school for several years before Bar Mitzvah or Bat Mitzvah to learn about Jewish holidays, language, customs, and history. He will also learn how to read the Torah and recite the attendant prayers.

The Bar Mitzvah happens automatically without the need for a ceremony to mark it. Nevertheless, Bar Mitzvah ceremonies, which were introduced in the last century, have become more and more popular among Jews. Not only do they mark the stage when a child becomes an adult in the eyes of the Jewish community, they also provide an opportunity for extended family members who stay far apart to come together and celebrate.

During the ceremony, the young person who is the Bar Mitzvah or Bat Mitzvah chants blessings, recites the *haftarah*, which is a section of Jewish scripture containing the writings of the Prophets, and reads the Torah portion of the week. A special meal is served during this occasion, which may take place in synagogues or at sites of historical or religious significance in Israel, such as the Western Wall, Southern Wall, or Masada.

For most Jews, this coming of age is an important and memorable part of their lives.

at home in the presence of at least 10 people. A pair of godparents is officially involved in the *brit*; the godfather (usually one of the grandfathers), who holds the baby, is designated the *sandak* (sahn-DAHK) and the godmother, who hands the baby to him is the *sandakit* (sahn-DAH-kit). Relatives and friends attend the *brit*, and a celebration takes place immediately after the ceremony.

There are no initiation rites for girls, although modern Jews feel strongly that there should also be rites for Jewish girls. The father announces the name that has been chosen for his daughter in the synagogue in a blessing ceremony. This is usually done on the sabbath after the child's birth. In some synagogues, the baby's name may be inscribed on a parchment to mark the occasion of her naming.

RELIGION

THE DECLARATION OF INDEPENDENCE of the state of Israel guarantees freedom of worship and the safety of the holy places of all religions. And partly because Jerusalem played a key role in the development of three of the world's major religions, different religious traditions are observed in Israel today.

Judaism is the majority religion in Israel. The religion forms the basic values on which the political structure of the government and Israel's nationhood are based.

Some of the other religions practiced in Israel include Islam, Christianity, and Baha'ism.

Opposite: **The Dome of the Rock Mosque in Jerusalem.**

Left: **The menorah engraved into a slab of basalt taken from one of many ancient Jewish synagogues. This slab dates back to the second century A.D.**

JUDAISM

"Hear, O Israel, the Lord our God, the Lord is One." This prayer is the fundamental message of Judaism. It refers to the covenant, or sacred agreement, that Jews will worship only one God and obey His laws. There is no priestly class between God and humanity, so Jews can appeal to God for help and praise Him directly.

In Judaism, it is a person's relationship with God that is stressed. The rabbi is the person in the community who is responsible for religious education, guidance, and services in the synagogue. His or her position does not involve special privileges. Rabbis interpret Jewish law and guide the spiritual lives of the people.

In the covenant, contained in the first five books of the Bible that are known as the Torah, God chose the descendants of Abraham to bring knowledge and acceptance of Him to the world. Through this acceptance, the Torah says, all of humanity can have a place in heaven.

The Talmud, another collection of authoritative ancient writings, combines with the Torah to form the religious laws that govern the lives of the Jewish people. These laws include ideas about the equality and rights of all people, personal morality, and personal freedom.

Judaism focuses on the works of God throughout the past, present, and future rather than on fixed formulas of belief. The focus on the past is through the study of the Jewish holy scripture; the present through living according to Jewish laws; and the future in anticipation of the coming Messiah.

Jewish laws are primarily concerned with moral values, teaching that people must be fair and kind to others, and that they should live a good life for the sake of being a good human being. The primary goal of Jewish law is to fulfill God's commandments.

BRANCHES OF JUDAISM

Until the 19th century, there was only one approach to Jewish religious tradition. Judaism was practiced in the way that is called Orthodox Judaism. Today, there are other branches of Judaism, such as Reform, Conservative, and Reconstructionist Judaism.

Orthodox means "the right way." People who adhere to this form of Judaism fully accept God's word as it was revealed to Moses in the Torah. Orthodox Jews strictly adhere to the Talmud and the later laws of the rabbis.

Strict observance of the sabbath, *kashrut* (KAHSH-root), or dietary law, and holy days are characteristics of Orthodox Judaism. Synagogue services are conducted exclusively in Hebrew. Married women wear head coverings at all times as evidence of modesty. Men and women are separated during worship in an Orthodox synagogue.

Reform Judaism rejects many of the practices and beliefs of Orthodox Judaism, including the authority of the Talmud and dietary laws. The Reform movement began in Germany in the early 1800s when some Jews felt that they needed to lead their lives in a way that was closer to the lifestyles of the non-Jewish people around them.

In Reform Judaism, head coverings are optional, and women and men worship together. Women can even become rabbis. The religious service is usually conducted in the native language of the worshipers (in the United States, for example, English is used frequently in the service).

Conservative Judaism also started in the 19th century. Followers agree with the practices of Reform Judaism, but are more moderate on certain religious issues. For example, they retain many Jewish traditions while recognizing the need for changes and adaptation to modern life. Although head coverings are required in the synagogue, men and women worship together and services are conducted both in Hebrew and the native language of the worshipers.

Reconstructionists see Judaism as a civilization, with the synagogue functioning as the center for all aspects of Jewish community life. The Reconstructionist service is similar to that of Conservative Judaism: men and women worship together. Women may also become rabbis. Reconstructionism is not widely practiced in Israel.

The stylish Heidal Yehuda Synagogue in Tel Aviv.

THE SYNAGOGUE

The Jewish house of worship is the synagogue or temple. It is considered the house of God and His people, or a place of assembly for people in the presence of God.

Modern synagogues have an auditorium where worshipers gather; a pulpit, or *bimah* (BEE-mah), above which hangs an electric light that is never switched off to symbolize the eternal light of the Torah; and a Holy Ark, where the scrolls of the Torah, the holiest scriptures, are kept.

Synagogues must have windows, for they are considered retreats for life rather than retreats from life. Many temples have a washbasin and pitcher in the lobby, so that worshipers can pour water over their hands as an act of cleansing. All synagogues face toward Jerusalem.

THE TORAH AND THE TALMUD

The word *Torah* means to teach in Hebrew. The Torah consists of the first five books of the Old Testament. Also known as the Pentateuch, the Torah is made up of the books of Genesis, Exodus, Leviticus, Numbers, and Deuteronomy, and contains the entire body of traditional Jewish religious teaching and study. Moses is credited with writing the Torah, having received inspiration from God at Mount Sinai.

In the synagogue, the Torah is in the form of a parchment scroll and is considered sacred. It is covered by highly decorated rich fabric.

The Talmud is a collection of 63 books of writings of ancient rabbis and discussions of the classification of religious and civil law by generations of scholars. It is also concerned with every aspect of Jewish life because Jewish religion and community are so closely related. There are two versions of the Talmud: the Palestinian Talmud and the Babylonian Talmud.

CHRISTIANITY

The Christians of Israel represent several branches of Christendom and live mainly in the towns of Jerusalem, Bethlehem, Nazareth, Haifa, and Yafo. Among the most common Christian communities in Israel are the Eastern Orthodox, Roman Catholic, Armenian, Eastern Catholic, Syrian Orthodox, and Evangelical.

As a rule, each community is headed by a patriarch or archbishop who is assisted by an advisory council. Israel's Christian communities have their headquarters in Jerusalem, where the revered Church of the Holy Sepulcher is located. This house of worship is equally sacred to all Christian denominations, but it is mainly controlled by the Armenian, Greek Orthodox, and Roman Catholic churches.

The most ancient church group in the Holy Land is the Greek Orthodox, which emerged before the middle of the second century. It gained importance during the reign of Emperor Constantine from 324 to 337 A.D.

Israeli Christians gather on Easter Sunday in Jerusalem.

87

A Muslim kneels in prayer.

ISLAM

Islam is the religion of Muslims, who make up the second largest religious group in Israel. According to Islamic belief, the angel Gabriel appeared to the Prophet Muhammad and told him to teach God's words to the world. Muhammad, who preached in the seventh century that there is only one God and that he (Muhammad) was the final messenger of God. His companions memorized and recorded his revelations. These eventually became the holy writings of the Koran.

Muslims believe in only one God (whom they call Allah), that Muhammad is His prophet, and that there will be a judgment day. Muslims pray five times a day facing the holy city of Mecca in Saudi Arabia. Prayer time is announced by a crier, or *muezzin* (moo-EH-zin), from a tower in the mosque. The head of the mosque is an *imam* (i-MAHM), who leads people in prayer.

The mosque is the most important building for Muslims. The word mosque comes from the Arabic word *masjid* (MAHS-jid), or place of prostration to God. Within the mosque, there is a *mihrab* (MIH-rahb), or prayer niche that points toward Mecca, a pulpit for the preacher, and a reading stand on which the Koran is placed. Most mosques have a minaret, a courtyard for washing before prayer, and a *madrasah* (MAH-drah-sah), or school.

Drinking liquor, gambling, and eating pork are forbidden in Islam. During the holy month of Ramadan, adult Muslims must go without eating or drinking from sunrise to sunset. A pilgrimage to Mecca is required at least once in a person's lifetime. Charity is also a requirement; Muslims must give a certain percentage of their wealth or income to the needy.

Like all religions, Islam has sects. Most Israeli Muslims belong to the Sunni sect. They believe that after Muhammad's death, leadership passed to the successors of Muhammad's clan. Shi'a Muslims, the second largest sect, believe that leadership passed on to the descendants of Muhammad's son-in-law.

THE KORAN

The sacred scriptures of Islam were written in Arabic and are collectively called the Koran. It contains 114 chapters called *surah* (SOO-rah) that serve as a guide on a wide range of issues, from various aspects of life to the universe and its Creator. The Koran is a timeless source of guidance for Muslims, and it is studied wherever Islam exists.

It is believed that the first official edition of the Koran appeared around A.D. 650. A copy was sent to each mosque in the capital cities of the Islamic world.

As an ancient sacred scripture, the Koran is highly symbolic. Its translation into other languages cannot reproduce the exact nuance or the appropriate sense, so those who would really like to understand the Koran have to learn Arabic first.

DRUZE

The Druze derive their name from Muhammad al-Darazi, a founder of the sect. While this community speaks Arabic and their outward social and cultural patterns are not too different from those of other people, they are distinguished by a strong sense of loyalty and unity. There is an effective ban on intermarriage and conversion of non-Druze to the sect that further separates this community from other Arabs. The Druze faction originated around 1000 B.C. but only gained official recognition in Israel in 1957.

Druze is an offshoot of Islam with beliefs and rituals that remain largely secret. It is known, however, that the people believe in a god that operates through a system of five cosmic principles and that there are periodic human appearances of the deity.

The Druze divide members of their faith into two groups: those who know the beliefs completely and those who do not. The first group consists of fewer than 10 percent of the total Druze population.

BAHA'I

The Baha'i faith was established in the mid-1800s in what is now Iraq. The efforts of Mirza Ali Muhammad, a 19th-century Persian mystic, are the inspiration behind this religion.

According to the Baha'i, a series of prophets were sent to teach moral truths and social principles. The last of these prophets was Baha'u'llah. Baha'u'llah proclaimed the importance of all religions worshiping one God and that service to other human beings is the most significant act. He also said that God wants a united society based on mutual love and acceptance, and stressed moral and social improvement.

The international governing body of the faith, the Universal House of Justice, meets in Haifa.

THE DEAD SEA SCROLLS

In 1947, a young Bedouin shepherd who was exploring a cave made one of the greatest archeological finds in history. In this cave in the cliffs overlooking the Dead Sea, he found a set of parchment and papyrus scrolls containing religious writings that had been preserved in earthenware jars for more than 2,000 years.

The recovered documents, now known as the Dead Sea Scrolls, were written by the ancient Hebrews who lived on what is now the site of Qumran. Thought to be members of the Essene sect, this devoutly religious group hid its sacred writings in the cave in anticipation of war with the Romans around A.D. 66. The Essene community was destroyed, but its writings remained, safely hidden through the ages.

After the initial discovery, archeological digs unearthed additional scrolls and fragments in 11 other caves. Years of study and careful reconstruction revealed the history of a community that removed itself from typical Jewish life, following a "teacher of righteousness" into the wilderness.

The scrolls tell much about the history of Jews, Christianity, and the Bible. Some were written in the sacred language of Hebrew, while others were written in Aramaic. Approximately one-fourth of the scrolls are biblical writings; each book of the Old Testament, except the book of Esther, is represented. A complete copy of the book of Isaiah was found, and it is believed to be the oldest copy.

The Dead Sea Scrolls are currently housed at the Shrine of the Book in Jerusalem, a museum devoted to these manuscripts. Access to the scrolls have long been the subject of controversy.

However, in 1990, two scholars from the Hebrew Union College in Cincinnati in the United States published a volume of computer-generated reconstruction of the scroll text. This edition, made from photographic negatives of the scrolls that recently became available at the Huntington Library in California, was made available to all qualified scholars. Losing their monopoly on the texts, the Israeli Antiquities Authority subsequently agreed to allow members of the public to see the scrolls.

LANGUAGE

ISRAEL HAS TWO OFFICIAL LANGUAGES: Hebrew and Arabic. Hebrew is the mother tongue of approximately 60 percent of the population. Arabic is spoken by many older Jews from Arab countries, and Yiddish by older Ashkenazim and Ultra-Orthodox Jews.

Arabic is taught in Israel's Arab schools and used in legal affairs and in the legislature. French is also taught in most schools. English is a *lingua franca* in Israel, which means that it is used as a common or commercial language among people who do not speak the same language. In fact, money, postage stamps, and road signs are printed in English as well as in Hebrew and Arabic, and English is a compulsory subject in schools. Very few Israelis speak only one language.

Opposite: **A religious Jew reads from the Torah.**

Left: **Even fast food has gone Hebrew. A Wendy's restaurant in Israel.**

A farmer takes time off from working the fields to read Hebrew.

HEBREW

Hebrew is one of the world's oldest languages. For over 2,000 years Hebrew has been the religious language of Jews and, at times, their spoken language. There are two main branches of Hebrew, Ashkenasic from Central Europe, and Sephardic from the Mediterranean region. The difference between the two is how each pronounces certain letters. Sephardic Hebrew is used in Israel.

Like any language, Hebrew has undergone changes throughout its history, but unlike most, there were not many changes until the modern period. The main reason for this is that Hebrew was not spoken, except in prayer, from the time the Jews were driven from Israel in the second century until the beginning of the 20th century.

Although the spoken language has changed by acquiring the thousands of words needed to become functional in the modern world, the written language has remained quite unchanged. In fact, today's Israeli high-school student can easily read and understand the original text of the Bible. The revival of Hebrew after 1,800 years of inactivity was due largely to the enormous work of Eliezer Ben-Yehuda, who emigrated to Israel in 1881.

ELIEZER BEN-YEHUDA Ben-Yehuda was responsible for the relentless task of creating modern words from ancient Hebrew roots. But without the cooperation of the Jews of Palestine, who eventually began to speak the language, Hebrew would have remained only a scriptural language.

THE HEBREW ALPHABET

The Hebrew alphabet consists of 22 letters, five of which have a different form when they appear at the end of a word. It is quite different from the English alphabet, for it has no capital letters or vowels.

In the eighth century, a system was developed for indicating vowels through the use of dots and dashes. These signs, called diacritics, are found in all printed editions of the Hebrew Bible.

Only when a word is part of a sentence can the reader know the intended meaning. Hebrew, like most Semitic languages, is read from right to left.

Cooperation was slow in coming, however. At first, Orthodox rabbis denounced the attempt as dishonoring the scriptures, and Zionist leader Theodor Herzl felt that speaking the language was not practical. But because language is closely tied to a culture's identity, the Jews of the world who were returning to their homeland finally accepted that Hebrew would be a unifying force. What made the acceptance of Hebrew successful was that Ben-Yehuda adapted the ancient written language for modern use. This allowed the millions of present and future immigrants to master the language easily and quickly.

Ben-Yehuda published a Hebrew newspaper and a 16-volume standard dictionary. In addition, he gathered a group of scholars to form a council, known today as the Hebrew Language Academy, or Vaad Ha-Lashon, to develop modern words. The academy continues to search the Bible and ancient Hebrew texts for words they can adapt to modern meanings. For example, for the word babysitter, they combined the words young child and guard.

When Ben-Yehuda started speaking Hebrew just over 100 years ago, it had a limited vocabulary. Today, Hebrew consists of more than 100,000 words, largely because of the tireless efforts of the Vaad Ha-Lashon. Words borrowed from other languages have also greatly contributed to the Hebrew lexicon.

Road signs to the Dead Sea in Hebrew, Arabic, and English.

ARABIC

Arabic is the mother tongue of about 300 million Middle Eastern people, spoken in a broad belt from the Arabian Peninsula all the way to the Atlantic Ocean. It is the language of Islam and the Koran and, in 1974, was named the sixth official language of the United Nations.

Hebrew and Arabic are languages in the Semitic language family. They have similar alphabet systems and word and sentence constructions.

Spoken Arabic varies across countries and may be mutually unintelligible. However, classical Arabic (the language of the Koran) has remained essentially unchanged since the seventh century and provides a common platform for Arabic-speaking people of different countries to communicate.

The alphabet consists of 28 letters, which are basically consonants. Vowel signs, as in Hebrew, are indicated by marks above and below the letters. Typical of Semitic languages, Arabic is read from right to left.

YIDDISH

Yiddish, spoken by many older Ashkenazim Israelis until approximately 50 years ago, was the language of the Jews of Eastern and Central Europe. It is a German dialect that is written in Hebrew characters. Vowels, however, are written in Yiddish.

. This language arose around the ninth century as Jews adapted German to their needs by adding Hebrew words that were a part of their religious life. As Jews migrated eastward, Yiddish picked up Slavic influences. It greatly reflects its culture: there are few terms descriptive of nature, which Eastern European Jews had little contact with, and it is loaded with descriptive terms of character and about relations between people. Yiddish continues to be spoken by Ultra-Orthodox Jews in Israel as they feel it is wrong to use Hebrew as an everyday language.

ISRAELI NAMES

A clear indication of how Hebrew has come to represent the Zionist spirit is evident in Israeli names. So eager were many Jews to become a part of their homeland that they took new Hebrew last names. Those who were able to translate their names into Hebrew did so.

A plaque in the Israel Museum in Jerusalem.

People named Schneider (German for "tailor") became Hayati; Weiss (white in German) was changed to Livni. Others chose last names representing their favorite regions, such as Galili (Galilee), Negbi (Negev), or Yerushalmi (Jerusalem).

Many newcomers selected names symbolic of their self-image or after their parents or children. Avigad is a common Israeli last name that simply means father of Gad. Eliezer Ben-Yehuda was Eliezer Perelman before emigrating to Palestine. Here, he preferred to be known as son of Judea. Ami, Avi, Bat, or Ben at the beginning of last names mean mother of, father of, daughter of, and son of respectively.

Others who took Hebrew surnames included prime ministers such as David Ben-Gurion (who was previously David Green) and Golda Meir (Goldie Meyerson). Ben-Gurion felt so strongly about this that he made changing of names to Hebrew a requirement for public servants and government officials.

Biblical first names such as Benjamin, Naomi, Esther, David, and Ezra remain popular. However, many people are naming their children after beautiful Hebrew words. Names such as Ayala (deer), Dafna (laurel), Orli (my light), Ari (lion), Eitan (strong, firm), and Gad (fortune) are also popular among Jews.

ARTS

Contemporary Israeli art is the product of many diverse cultural influences. These stem from a rising non-Jew—largely Arab—segment of the Israeli population as well as from returning Jews who bring back with them ideas, values, and perspectives that they have acquired through having lived for decades in countries all over the world.

The first known work of Jewish literature is, of course, the Bible. Jewish art and architecture also date back to ancient times. From the time Moses asked Bezalel to craft a gold menorah and an ark for the Ten Commandments, the Jewish people have made beautiful jewelry, pottery, and on a larger scale temples and castles.

Opposite: **Israeli painter Reuven Spiers working in his gallery.**

Left: **Chalices, goblets, cooking pots, oil lamps, and baking trays found in the ruins of Tel Kadesh Barnea in the Negev Desert. The town was a frontier fort for the southern part of King Solomon's kingdom in the 10th century B.C.**

The Jerusalem Theater.

THE PERFORMING ARTS

Music has contributed greatly to the cultural advancement and international reputation of Israel. The Israel Philharmonic Orchestra, founded in 1936, has had many famous musicians and conductors among its ranks. These include Isaac Stern and Itzak Perlman, two violinists who are known the world over for their musical talent. Israelis are tremendously devoted to the Philharmonic Orchestra. It is one of the most widely supported orchestras (per capita) in the world. It is said that residents of Tel Aviv read the obituaries in hopes of recognizing the name of someone they knew who happened to be a ticket holder!

Israel's music in the early years of statehood was very much in the folk tradition, with a biblical focus. It has since gone away from the religious and toward the political. Described as sad but optimistic, it touches on the things that are on the minds of the Israelis, such as peace and war.

The many cultural groups that have come together have blended to create a musical form that is distinctly Israeli. One popular singer, Ofra Haza, even recorded a 16th-century Yemenite prayer, sung to rap music; it sold more than a million albums worldwide.

Israelis also love the theater. There are five major acting companies in the country, and Israelis lead the world in per capita theater attendance. Habima, the national theater company, has been producing plays since 1932. It performs three times daily, six days a week, to near capacity crowds. Beersheba, Jerusalem, and Haifa have repertory acting companies, and community theaters flourish throughout the land, including on the *kibbutz*.

LITERATURE

There has been a continuous Hebrew literary tradition even though the language was not spoken, except in religious services, from the second century until the late 19th century.

Most literary works that emerged soon after Israel was created in 1948 were by writers who took part in the Palmach, an elite strike force set up in 1941. These writers wrote about war and heroism. Haim Gouri and Moshe Shamir are among the writers who belong to this generation.

Israeli literature addressed personal issues in the 1950s and 1960s, as writers such as Amos Oz, Aaron Applefeld, and A. B. Yehoshua reflected on the struggles of individuals and families in a young state, the Holocaust, and the gathering and absorbing of Jews of various ethnic groups in Israel. S. Y. Agnon, perhaps the best-known writer of this group, won the 1966 Nobel Prize for Literature for his fictional works.

The 1980s saw a revolution in Israeli literature. A large number of young writers emerged with original works during this period, and there was a greater variety of books from different and new genres.

Postmodern literary works have moved away from taking moral or ideological stands, and resemble the Western style of writing.

As works by Israeli Arab writers are usually in Arabic, they have not joined the mainstream body of literature in Israel, most of which are in Hebrew. Their works have not gone uncredited, however. Emil Habibi is an Israeli Arab writer who won the Israel Prize, while Anton Shammas is an Israeli Christian Arab recognized for his 1986 *Arabesques*, one of the first Israeli Arab literary works.

Over the past six decades, Israeli literature has evolved from focusing on ideological and Zionist issues to addressing personal experiences and later abstract postmodernist concerns.

VISUAL ARTS

Israelis are fond of art, and an original artwork can usually be found in even the smallest apartment. There are countless art galleries in the cities—especially Tel Aviv—and for a country of its size, Israel has many museums. These museums are found in cities and even on the *kibbutz*, housing treasures of archeology and local history, ancient and modern artworks, and primitive and sophisticated craftworks.

An attempt at an Israeli style in painting was started by the Bezalel School of Arts and Crafts, which was founded in Jerusalem in 1906. The style combined traditional Jewish themes and images with modern Western concepts, but over the years, newness and originality have been the major element in Israeli art. The result is that there is no single identifiable Israeli "school" of art.

ISRAEL'S FIRST ART SCHOOL

The Bezalel School of Arts and Crafts in Jerusalem was founded by sculptor Boris Schatz. His aim was to foster a connection between the Jewish people and handwork. Schatz's goal was not to promote and present the art of the Israelis, but to encourage the creation of original art.

The Bezalel School struggled financially in its early years, and in 1928 lost the struggle. It remained shut until 1935 when painter Joseph Budko, along with European artists and teachers who emigrated to Israel, re-opened the school.

The school has offered programs in all areas of arts and craft, and Israel's most respected artists have attended the institution. Teachers from all over the world are among the faculty at the school, which in the late 1960s attained the status of Academy of Arts and Design. It is now considered the supreme arts institution in Israel.

There have been a few art movements in Israel. New Horizons dedicated itself to the advancement of abstract tendencies in the 1950s. "102" was established some time later, but the artists of these movements remained true to their individuality.

In recent years, Israeli artwork has been exhibited at the Jewish Museum in New York. The show, called *Artists of Israel: 1920–1980*, included pieces by well-known artists such as Reuven Rubin, Tziona Tagger, Yosef Zaritsky, and Yaakov Agam.

A younger generation of work was also represented, and the number of successful women artists shows that there is equal opportunity in the arts in Israel. Artist communities, run on a cooperative basis, are located near Haifa and in Old Jaffa.

DANCE

Dance has always been an integral part of Jewish life. There are many biblical references to it as an expression of joy and religious excitement, and the Jews have incorporated dance into many types of ceremonies.

The various ethnic groups that have emigrated to the Holy Land brought many dance forms, among them the *debka* (DAB-kah), which is an Arabic line dance performed by men, and the *hora* (HORE-uh), an Eastern European circle dance. In many traditional dances, there is strict separation of the sexes in dance, so participants hold the ends of a handkerchief to prevent physical contact.

Community folk dancing is a part of modern Israeli culture. After the sabbath on Saturday evenings, Israelis join in folk dancing in local parks and on the *kibbutzim*. Professional dance groups are heavily supported in Israel. There are three major modern dance institutions, professional folk-dance groups, and even a hearing-impaired dancers' troupe.

Artists perform at the Arts & Crafts Fair, which is held every Tuesday and Friday at the Nachalat Benjamin Street, Tel Aviv.

THE INBAL DANCE THEATER

The Inbal Dance Theater celebrates traditions of the Yemenite Jews, who were isolated from mainstream Judaism for 2,000 years. The music and dance forms that the Yemenite Jews brought to their new home are reminders of ancient religious rituals and ceremonies.

Yemenite music and storytelling accompany the traditional dance movements, which include rhythmic walking, exciting head and body movements, and captivating hand gestures.

ARCHITECTURE

In Israel, all styles of architecture combine. From the traditional Arab-style villas that blend into the surrounding landscape and the simple tile-roofed houses of the first settlers to the modern European forms of seaside cottages.

After the post-World War I and post-World War II mass immigrations, the *shikkun* (shi-KOON), or housing project, became necessary to accommodate the increase in population, with an emphasis on usefulness rather than beauty. Nonetheless, since statehood, Israeli architects have attempted to introduce style and grace into new institutions. Higher education campuses led the way in the creation of structures with a style that could be characterized as Israeli; the Hebrew University Givat Ram campus in Jerusalem, the Technion in Haifa, and the Weizmann Institute in Rehovot are all examples of beautifully designed, highly functional buildings.

Other public buildings with notable architecture are the Israel Museum Complex in Jerusalem, the Knesset, concert halls, and the Jerusalem and Haifa theaters.

LEISURE

THE LEISURE ACTIVITIES OF THE ISRAELI PEOPLE are influenced by a few very important factors. First of all, there is little leisure time. Israelis work and go to school six days a week. Their one day off is the sabbath, when many businesses are closed and public transportation does not run. Added to this is the fact that the typical Israeli has little money for recreation after all the bills are paid.

The most popular leisure activity in Israel is visiting. On weekday evenings, people visit friends and family. Adults get together quite often for coffee and cake. On Friday evenings, even the least religious of Jewish families have their version of the traditional sabbath dinner.

Opposite: **Israeli children kayaking at Kibbutz Sdot Yam beach.**

Left: **Youths having a picnic by the Jordan River.**

IN PURSUIT OF LEISURE

There is a strong emphasis on physical fitness in Israel, as most Jewish citizens serve in the military for a few years and remain on call for reservist training for some time after. So sports and outdoor or nature activities such as hiking are popular leisure pursuits.

Much of the Israelis' free time is spent outdoors. People love to go out to eat. Food vendors are everywhere, offering a variety of international fast foods from the Middle Eastern *falafel* (fuh-LAH-fehl), or spicy ground chickpea balls, to New York-style hot dogs. Outdoor cafés are very popular. While enjoying a cup of iced coffee, many people get together to play chess and backgammon or argue about politics and world affairs.

As in any country, some of the types of leisure activities that the inhabitants enjoy are determined by locality.

Some interests that are shared by all Israelis are reading, going to the movies, watching television, listening to the radio, and attending concerts and the ballet.

SPORTS

Sports have become increasingly important in Israel in recent years. There are many sports clubs as well as facilities and equipment provided for the population by both the government and private organizations.

Soccer is by far Israel's favorite sport; all activity seems to stop on the afternoon of an important soccer match. Spectators tend to become quite involved in the game, especially if they do not agree with an important decision by the referee. Israel has a soccer team that competes internationally and a national league, in which teams compete against one another on a regular basis.

Basketball is growing in popularity. One Israeli team, Maccabi Tel Aviv, has twice captured the European Cup championship. There is also a 12-team professional league with many U.S.-born players.

Interest in tennis is growing by leaps and bounds. The country's climate is perfect for outdoor activity throughout the year, and there are tennis courts and stadiums in most cities and towns. Two Israeli professional tennis players, Shlomo Glickstein and Amos Mansdorf, have been ranked among the top competitors in the world.

Hiking is a great national passion. On Saturday afternoons, countless families pack into their cars and set out for national parks for a picnic and to explore the country on foot. An organized annual springtime hiking event that is a three-day march through the hills of Judea and Samaria has attracted participants ranging from teenagers to people in their 70s. Those who finish the march parade victoriously through Jerusalem.

Desert hikers stop by a pool for a rest.

THE MACCABIAH GAMES

In 2001 Israel again hosted the Maccabiah Games, an Olympics-style sporting event for Jewish athletes from around the world. The goal of the games is to bring Jews together in the Holy Land and to promote physical excellence and well-being.

Joseph Yekutieli founded the Maccabiah Games in 1932. In the first games, approximately 500 athletes from 23 countries participated, and many later remained in Palestine to become citizens. For the second Maccabiah Games in 1935, nearly 2,000 athletes came. However, the third games did not take place until 1950, first postponed because of World War II, and later due to the establishment of the state of Israel.

Today, the Maccabiah Games are held in Israel every four years. Events include table tennis, basketball, volleyball, track and field, tennis, boxing, soccer, swimming, water polo, gymnastics, fencing, and wrestling.

Like the Olympics, the Maccabiah Games have dramatic and moving opening and closing ceremonies, which are attended by top Israeli officials.

TELEVISION

Israelis love to watch television not just for entertainment but for newscasts that provide important information for a country where dramatic events occur often. The length of the newscast depends on the amount of news, but on an average day, it runs for 30 minutes. Apart from the news, Israelis enjoy the same type of television entertainment as do North Americans. In fact, much of Israeli television fare is imported from the United States.

Israeli television is mainly broadcast on one channel. Popular Israeli programs include *Zu Artzaynu*, or *This is Our Country*, a late-night satire of politics and current affairs. *Shemesh* is Israel's longest-running sitcom which centers on life in a café in Tel Aviv. Educational programs, such as the Hebrew version of *Sesame Street*, and cartoons are aired from morning until about 5 P.M.

Arabic television follows the educational broadcasts. For three hours, the Israeli Arab minority, residents of the occupied territories, and any Arab in the neighboring countries who is interested, tune in to the Arabic news and other Arabic programs. Israelis can also watch Jordanian and Syrian television, because the Middle Eastern electronic media have no national boundaries.

American programs are very popular and are aired after the Arabic programs. Israeli TV also imports programs from Europe, Canada, and Australia. There are no commercials on Israeli TV.

There is another television station known as The Second Channel, but its broadcasts are limited, and in some areas a special antenna is required to receive the channel. American news programs such as *Nightline*, *The McNeil-Lehrer Report*, and *Cable News Network* are carried on this station.

Cable television has become available to Israelis, putting them in touch with television stations all over the world. Video tapes are also popular. In cities and towns throughout the country, no matter how small or religious, there are video stores with large selections of movies.

RADIO

Radio is also an Israeli passion. Bus drivers turn up the volume of the hourly newscasts so that passengers can hear all the latest news; and during times of great crisis, Israelis are never without radios by their side.

Israel has a major news station that employs the finest journalists, who are constantly interviewing top Israeli officials such as the prime minister and giving reports and commentaries on economic and international news. There is also a military radio station that not only presents four newscasts daily, but also jazz and rock music.

The Israeli Broadcasting Authority broadcasts programs for local and overseas listeners in 16 languages, including Hebrew, Arabic, English, French, Russian, and Spanish. It gears its programming to the needs of Israel's immigrants. The musical tastes of the young and old are also satisfied. One station beats out rock tunes all day long and into the night, while another dedicated to classical music soothes thousands with its 18 hours of broadcasting each day.

One of the balloons in the International Hot Air Balloon Competition at Arad near the Dead Sea.

FESTIVALS

THE WORD FESTIVAL brings to mind a joyous celebration. However, many major festivals have a serious reason behind them, and some of the rituals and practices associated with these festivals create a somber mood as people commemorate major historical events. In Israel, the holy land of three of the world's great religions, people celebrate festivals that range from religious to secular and from solemn to cheerful.

THE LUNAR CALENDAR

Israelis live their daily lives by a solar calendar that starts with the month of January and ends with December. This is known as the Gregorian calendar. However, Israelis mark the dates of their national and religious holidays on a lunar calendar that starts with the month of Tishri and ends with Elul. This is known as the Hebrew calendar. If the date is May 31, 2003, on the Gregorian calendar, it is Iyar 29, 5763, on the Hebrew calendar. *The Jerusalem Post* tells you both the Gregorian and the Hebrew dates every day.

The 12 Hebrew months begin with the appearance of the new moon, and each month has 29 or 30 days. To prevent the lunar year from slipping too far behind the solar year, every few years an extra month, called Adar Bet or Adar II, is added.

The Islamic calendar also has 12 months that begin with the new moon. However, it does not make an attempt to relate the lengths of the solar and lunar years, and a holiday that occurs in summer one year can fall in winter years later. If a Gregorian date, let's say May 31, falls in the Islamic month of Rabi-ul-Awwal in the year 2003 (1424 on the Islamic calendar), the same date would have fallen in a different Islamic month, Zil-Hajj, a decade earlier, in 1993 (1413 on the Islamic calendar).

Following a lunar year schedule can have some very interesting results. For example, when Israel celebrated its independence on May 14 in 1948, it was the fifth day of the Hebrew month of Iyar, which will not coincide with May 14 again until the year 2005.

Opposite: **Israeli girls take part in Independence Day celebrations in Herzlia.**

JEWISH HOLIDAYS

Since ancient times, Jews have cherished and observed their holy days. The rituals were a uniting force for the Jews of the Diaspora, and the holidays themselves served as reminders of their strong leadership and exceptional circumstances. Some of the holidays celebrated in Israel originated more than 3,000 years ago. Over the years, when the Jews met great challenges, they added more memorable days to their festivals calendar.

THE HIGH HOLY DAYS

Rosh Hashanah and Yom Kippur mark the beginning of the Jewish year. According to tradition, God opens three books on Rosh Hashanah—one for the wicked, one for the righteous, and one for all others. The names of the righteous are written in the Book of Life; the wicked are designated for death in the coming year; and judgment on the rest is suspended for a 10-day period of personal accounting and atonement that occurs between Rosh Hashanah and Yom Kippur. A typical greeting among Jews during this holiday season is, "May you be inscribed in the Book of Life."

One highlight of Rosh Hashanah is when the ram's horn, or *shofar* (show-fahr), is trumpeted. For Jews everywhere, the *shofar* is a memorable symbol of the Jewish New Year.

ROSH HASHANAH falls in September or October. While the holiday has a serious overtone, the new year is welcomed with a sense of joy. After attending synagogue services, Jewish families gather for a festive meal. Jewish delicacies are prepared as symbols of good luck. The following night, fruits of the season are eaten for the first time in the new year. This holiday is extremely popular because it is the only one in the entire year that is observed for two consecutive days. Apart from worshiping, Israelis take advantage of the break by making trips to the beach, organizing picnics and barbecues, or hiking in the country's national parks.

YOM KIPPUR On Yom Kippur, Jews make their peace with God and their conscience. It is said that one's fate is written on Rosh Hashanah and sealed on Yom Kippur by God. Judgement is made after an appropriate period of soul-searching and asking for forgiveness from God.

Yom Kippur has been observed since the days of Moses. On this solemn day, Jews refrain from eating and drinking to atone for the sins of the past year. Their fast begins at sundown on the eve of Yom Kippur and ends at sundown on Yom Kippur with a large meal shared by the whole family.

SUKKOT

Shortly after the High Holy Days, traditional Jews celebrate Sukkot, the Harvest Festival, over a period of eight days. Families build a *sukkah* (SOO-kah), or hut, next to their homes, representing the dwelling of the ancient Jews who wandered the desert after their escape from Egypt.

Sukkot is the most visible festival in Israel. Even secular *kibbutznik* build the *sukkah*. In their case, however, the *sukkah* symbolizes the Diaspora. Israelis who celebrate the religious aspect of Sukkot eat their meals in the *sukkah* in thanksgiving at the close of the harvest season.

Simchat Torah (Rejoicing of the Torah) falls on the last day of Sukkot and is celebrated with dancing, singing, and worship. It coincides with the completion of the reading of the Torah for the year. In the synagogue, a parade precedes a ceremonial unrolling of a Torah scroll to the first chapter, and the reading of the first five books of the Bible begins anew.

A Jewish man lights candles on the *hanukkiah*. This is the most important ritual in Hanukkah celebrations.

HANUKKAH

Hanukkah is an eight-day festival that celebrates the victory of Judah Maccabee's warriors over the Syrians, who tried to convert their religion in the second century B.C. Upon victory, the Jews set out to rededicate the temple in Jerusalem, only to find that there was just enough oil to burn for one day. However, the oil miraculously burned for eight days.

To celebrate this miracle, Jews burn candles on the *hanukkiah*, a special menorah with nine candle holders used in Hanukkah celebrations. One candle is lit on each of the festival's eight nights. The ninth candle, called *shamash*, or servant candle, is the first to be lit and used for lighting all the other candles.

Hanukkah is enjoyed widely in Israel; families gather to party and eat traditional Hanukkah foods, and children receive gifts from their parents on each of the eight nights. In the village of Modin, where the Maccabees came from, a special relay race commemorates the holiday. The first runner lights the torch of freedom and independence and carries it to the next runner. The passing of the torch goes on until the last runner reaches Jerusalem and hands the torch to the president of Israel.

PESACH

Pesach, or Passover, a springtime holiday, is a memorial of the Israelites' escape from hundreds of years of slavery in Egypt.

An Orthodox Jewish family cleaning cooking utensils in preparation for Pesach, or Passover.

The word passover comes from the time when God sent an angel to slay the firstborn son of every Egyptian home, but passed over Jewish homes that were marked with blood from sacrificial lambs. The Egyptians were so overcome by the tragedy that the Jews were able to escape. The fleeing Jews had no time to wait for the bread they were baking to rise. Thus even today Jews observe a restriction against foods that rise and certain grains throughout Passover.

An important night during Pesach is the evening of the Seder, which is a ceremonial dinner on the first night of this seven-day festival. The Seder recreates the events of the escape, or exodus, from Egypt. A special storyline of the exodus called the *Hagadda* (HOG-ah-dah) is read aloud. Celebrants (especially children) participate by answering questions from the *Hagadda* and eating the symbolic foods for the ceremony.

This holiday is also celebrated by all Jews, as it is a festival of freedom. Yom HaShoah, the Holocaust Memorial, is celebrated after Passover. Shavuot, the day God gave the Ten Commandments to the Israelites, is celebrated after Israel's Memorial and Independence Day.

Followers of the Greek Orthodox Church of the Twelve Apostles assemble in a church at Capernaum by the Sea of Galilee.

MEMORIAL AND INDEPENDENCE

Independence Day celebrations are preceded by Memorial Day, when Israelis remember those who gave their lives for the state.

During Memorial Day, television and radio stations broadcast documentaries on Israeli battles and their heroes. During a two-minute silence, work stops while cars and buses wait at the side of the road. At sundown, sirens scream across the country and the Independence Day celebrations begin. Families build bonfires on the hillsides and people sit around the fires to sing and tell stories. Celebrants, especially children, participate by asking and answering questions from the *Hagadda* and eating the symbolic foods for the ceremony.

CHRISTIAN HOLIDAYS

Like Christians everywhere, Israeli Christians celebrate Christmas, Good Friday, and Easter. During these holidays, church bells in the old section of Jerusalem ring, summoning Christians to walk where Jesus walked.

At Christmas, pilgrims gather around Manger Square in Bethlehem, while beautiful music pours out of the Church of the Nativity. Christians also look out for Baba Noel, as Santa Claus is known in Israel, and decorate their houses with Christmas trees.

Easter offers the most dramatic sight in Jerusalem, where hundreds of pilgrims make their way down Via Dolorosa during Holy Week. This is the route Jesus took to Calvary, where he was crucified.

JEWISH FESTIVALS

Holiday	2003	Hebrew date
Tu B'Shvat (New Year for Trees)	Jan 18	Sh'vat 15, 5763
Purim (Feast of Lots)	Mar 18	Adar II 14, 5763
Pesach (Passover)	Apr 17–24	Nisan 15–22, 5763
Yom HaShoah (Holocaust Memorial Day)	Apr 29	Nisan 27, 5763
Yom HaZikaron (Israel's Memorial Day)	May 6	Iyar 4, 5763
Yom HaAtzma'ut (Israel Independence Day)	May 7	Iyar 5, 5763
Yom Yerushalayim (Jerusalem Day)	May 30	Iyar 28, 5763
Shavuot (Weeks)	Jun 6–7	Sivan 6–7, 5763
Rosh Hashanah 5764 (New Year)	Sep 27–28	Tishri 1–2, 5764
Yom Kippur (Day of Atonement)	Oct 6	Tishri 10, 5764
Sukkot (Festival of Tabernacles)	Oct 11–17	Tishri 15–22, 5764
Simchat Torah (Rejoicing of the Torah)	Oct 19	Tishri 23, 5764
Hanukkah (Festival of Lights)	Dec 19–27	Kislev 24–Tevet 2, 5764

ISLAMIC HOLIDAYS

The most joyous of Muslim holidays occurs at the end of the fasting month of Ramadan, when there is a three-day feast called Id-al-Fitr. It is also a time for family visits. Sweet pastries are served and children receive gifts such as clothing. People also dye their hands with a natural orange-red dye called henna as a symbol of good luck.

Id-al-Adha, the Feast of the Sacrifice, is also referred to as the "big holiday." It honors Ibrahim and his son Ismail. According to the Koran, God wanted to test Ibrahim's loyalty by commanding him to sacrifice his beloved son, Ismail. When Ibrahim relayed this command to Ismail, the latter encouraged his father to obey, out of their great love and faith in God. When the moment for Ismail's sacrifice came, however, God substituted a lamb in his place as a sign of His Grace and Power. Muslims sacrifice sheep, cows, or goats to remember this event. The meat is cooked in special festive dishes, with portions of it given to the poor. This holiday abounds with sweet pastries, henna, and gifts. Muslims who can afford it perform the pilgrimage to Mecca in Saudi Arabia during this period. This pilgrimage is one of the five pillars of Islam and should be performed at least once in a Muslim's lifetime according to the person's means.

FOOD

ISRAEL MAY BE A YOUNG NATION, but its cuisine has a long history. People from many parts of the world have settled in the country, bringing with them their favorite traditional recipes, which are perhaps centuries old. Blending these varied culinary traditions, Israelis have developed a cuisine that they can now call their own.

It would not have been clear back in the 1940s whether an Israeli cuisine would emerge. With many more urgent matters to think about, cooking styles and methods did not seem all that important; food was an essential, something people needed in order to survive and get by. Today, however, many Israelis enjoy the art and experience of cooking with an ethnic flair.

Opposite: **An Arab woman sells fresh fruit juices at the food market in Acco.**

Left: **Asian-style cakes for sale at a food market.**

ISRAELI FOODS

The foods eaten in Israel today are a blend of foods from many cultures. Native Israeli cuisine might be described as similar to that of the Arab nations, but the Asian and European influence on the Israeli diet is unmistakable. Asian cuisine brings with it the flavor and aroma of spices and herbs, while European cuisine is relatively sweeter. Israeli cuisine combines the two with modern recipes.

The Israeli food tradition was formed according to the availability (or lack) of certain foods. For example, fruits and vegetables, which are inexpensive and grown in large amounts, are included in virtually every meal. Dairy products, including different types of yogurt and soured milks and creams, are also a major part of the Israeli diet. Red meat is rarely eaten, partly because the lack of quality grazing land for livestock produces a lower grade of meat. Turkey and chicken are a major part of the Israeli diet.

The Jewish state's contribution to world cuisine is undoubtedly the Israeli breakfast. This outstanding meal has its roots in the *kibbutz*. In the early morning hours, *kibbutz* farmers have a light snack consisting of tea with toast and jam so that they can get to the fields before the day gets hot. It is after putting in a few hours of hard work that they return for breakfast.

A typical Israeli breakfast, especially on the *kibbutz*, consists of vegetables such as tomatoes, onions, green peppers, and radishes; olives; eggs; carrot salad; a variety of dairy products, including buttermilk, yogurt, cottage cheese, and hard cheeses; breads; herring; hot cereals; and coffee or tea. It is served buffet-style and satisfies everyone's appetite.

For other meals, *falafel* sandwiches are favorites. Typically Middle Eastern, *falafel* sandwiches are filled with fried balls of chickpeas mixed with garlic, onion, and spices. *Falafel* is usually served in pita bread, with tahini sauce (sesame seed paste) poured over the *falafel*.

Typical Israeli-Sephardic food, with some Asian influence.

Another dish enjoyed throughout Israel is *humus* (HOO-moos), a smooth paste of chickpeas with garlic and tahini sauce. Other Arabic foods that are quite popular among the people of Israel are *shawarma* (SHAH-wahr-mah), spicy sliced lamb or chicken usually served on pita; a marinated lamb dish called *shashlik* cooked on skewers over a flame; and shish kebab.

Cholent (CHOE-luhn) is a stew traditionally served on the Jewish sabbath, which is observed on Saturday. Because the oven in a religious home cannot be lit after sundown on Friday, *cholent* is a perfect meal. It simmers overnight in a warm oven turned on before the sabbath. Various types of *cholent* reflect the traditional foods of the different Jewish ethnic groups. Moroccan Jews, for example, use beef, spices, chickpeas, and potatoes, while Sephardic Jews include beans, meat, potatoes, and eggs.

Kugel (KOO-gehl), a noodle casserole that is a traditional food among Eastern European Jews, is also a sabbath favorite because it too can be left overnight in a warm oven and be ready for the meal on Saturday.

A fruit and vegetable vendor at the Tel Aviv Ha-Karmel market.

JEWISH DIETARY LAWS

Another factor that plays a significant role in the Israeli menu is the dietary law of the Jews and Muslims.

The *kashrut* is the kosher dietary system for Jews. Foods that are permitted are referred to as kosher, which means fit or proper. Those that are not are called *trefa* (treh-FAH). The dietary laws, which Jews have followed for thousands of years, are stated in the Bible and discussed extensively in the Talmud. Orthodox Jews believe that these laws are given by God and cannot be violated.

The *kashrut* falls into three categories: foods that can and cannot be eaten, the slaughter and preparation of meat, and the ways foods are served. (Since all *kashrut* rules involve animals, the Jewish vegetarian has little to worry about!)

The laws state that any animal with cloven or split hoofs that chews cud is edible; both criteria must be met. Therefore, lamb and beef are allowed, while rabbit, camel, and pork are not. Wild birds and birds of prey that seize food in their claws are unclean and therefore prohibited. Buzzards, cranes, eagles, and owls are not acceptable, but turkey, chicken, duck, and pigeon are. Fish that have fins and scales are clean and can be consumed, while those without, such as catfish, porpoise, shrimp, and lobster, are forbidden.

Animals and fowl that can be eaten must be slaughtered and prepared according to strict rules that include removing the veins and arteries from the carcass. The meat must then be soaked in water and salted.

Rules for serving food state that dairy products and meat must not be eaten together. This separation is maintained throughout preparation, cooking, and eating, and separate sets of dishes, cookware, and silverware are required.

ISLAMIC DIETARY LAWS

Muslims also have dietary laws that are spelled out in the Koan. Foods that are permitted are referred to as *halal* (hah-LULL). These laws are also about eating and slaughtering animals, and although they differ from the *kashrut*, they share some similarities. For example, consumption of blood and pork is prohibited. Food that is found dead or has been offered to idols is not edible for the Muslim and, as is the case with Jews, animals must be slaughtered according to a ritual. Muslims are also prohibited from drinking alcohol.

HOLIDAY FOODS

All areas of Israeli life are influenced by the festivals and holy days of the Jewish year. So too are the foods eaten, because the festivals marking the holidays are usually observed by eating certain foods.

ROSH HASHANAH The Jewish year begins in autumn with Rosh Hashanah. Traditionally, sweet foods such as apples and honey are eaten to remind Jews of the sweetness of God's blessings. A round loaf of bread called *challah* (CHAH-lah) is also consumed. The round bread reminds Jews that they are bound to the wheel of fate. People eat pieces dipped in honey to ensure a sweet year. Salads and sour foods are avoided; nothing should alter the sweetness of the beginning of the year.

Spices of all kinds can be found at this stall in an Israeli market.

YOM KIPPUR takes place 10 days after Rosh Hashanah. To atone for the sins of the past year, Jews eat no food from the hour before sunset on the eve of Yom Kippur until after sunset the next day. Bland chicken and rice is eaten before the fast to help prevent thirst and indigestion. Then a morsel of bread and water is taken as a symbolic gesture of nourishment. After the fast, families and friends eat together, starting with apple dipped in honey. Herring or other salty food follows. The rest of the meal consists of traditional foods of particular ethnic groups.

SUKKOT This eight-day harvest festival is marked by Orthodox Jews eating meals in the *sukkah*, a hut decorated with fruit which commemorates the huts that Jews lived in when they left Egypt and wandered in the desert for 40 years before entering Israel. Harvest foods such as figs, apricots, pomegranates, onions, barley, and lettuce are part of each meal.

Israeli date palms.

HANUKKAH The Festival of Lights is celebrated for eight days in the winter. It marks the time when a small amount of oil miraculously continued to burn in the rededicated temple in Jerusalem for eight days. Foods fried in oil, such as *latkes* (LAHT-kehs), or potato pancakes, and *sufganiyot* (soof-gah-ni-YOAT), or doughnuts, are enjoyed during this holiday.

PURIM Also known as the Feast of Esther, this springtime festival celebrates the story of Queen Esther saving the Jewish people from a murderous tyrant, Haman. People eat Haman's Ears, or *hamentashen* (HUH-muhn-tash), which are sweet cakes filled with prunes or poppy seeds. Wine is served, because Haman's defeat was due to the excessive amount of wine Esther served him. Traditional foods include chickpeas, *kreplach* (KREH-plah), or dumplings, and turkey.

Sufganiyot are jelly doughnuts eaten during Hanukkah.

PESACH, or Passover, celebrates the Jews' escape from Egypt. The fleeing Jews baked unleavened bread because they could not wait for the dough to rise. As a result, *matzo*, an unleavened cracker-like bread, is eaten. The first evening is marked by a ritual meal called a Seder, and for the remainder of the week, nothing leavened by yeast may be eaten. During the Seder, a special plate is prepared with foods recalling the trials of the Jews during the bitter years of Egyptian slavery. Foods include bitter herbs and hard-boiled eggs.

SHAVUOT This holiday is the last festival of the year. It celebrates Moses receiving the Ten Commandments and the summer fruits coming into season. Dairy dishes such as cheese blintzes (pancakes) are served. Accompanying the milk products are honey biscuits to celebrate Israel being "the land of milk and honey."

SABBATH takes place on the seventh day of every week, starting at sundown Friday and ending at sundown Saturday. It is a special day of rest and prayer. Like all Jewish celebrations, the sabbath, or shabat, has its special foods, the most common being the *challah*, or sabbath bread. Each family has its own special dishes that are enjoyed on the sabbath.

STREET FOODS

Israelis are always on the move, and because there is not much leisure time, people like to eat and run. Israel not only has a lively street vendor industry, it also has a booming gas station/fast-food trade. What started out as a convenience—filling up the gas tank and stomach at the same time—has turned cultural. People dodge traffic to run and grab some *mezze* (MEH-zeh), an appetizer; grilled meat or fish; and sweet Turkish coffee.

For pedestrians, *falafel* is found almost everywhere. In fact, after paying for the first *falafel* on pita, Israelis can have additional servings of the chickpea mixture while only paying for the pita.

Another tasty street food is *brik*, which is filo dough filled with cheese or potato. Bagels are sold warm on

A woman buys fresh produce at the Mahane Yehuda market.

street corners, and some vendors offer a tasty dip called *za'atar* (ZAH-ah-tahr). On the sweet side, a caramel-like custard called *malabi* (MAH-lah-bee) is eaten from little tin cups. *Tamarindi* (TAH-mah-reen-dee) is a favorite syrupy juice that street vendors carry in large jars on their shoulders. For fast food, hamburgers are available at MacDavid's, Israel's answer to McDonald's, and Burger Ranch. The similarities end there, however, because the hamburgers and hot dogs served in Israel are much spicier than those in the United States.

Perhaps the most common outdoor food is sunflower seeds. The experienced seed eater can remove the meat and spit out the shell without ever taking a hand to the mouth. Discarded shells line the sidewalks and roadways, making sunflower seeds the ultimate street food in Israel.

KASHA CHOLENT

This sabbath dish, prepared in advance for days when cooking is prohibited, is a hot meal for four to six people.

2 pounds beef brisket	$^1/_4$ teaspoon paprika (optional)
1 large onion, finely diced	$^1/_2$ teaspoon salt
1 cup navy beans or kidney beans	dash of pepper
1 cup coarse-milled buckwheat groats	water
1 cup grated raw carrot (optional)	

Brown the meat on all sides in a heavy pot. Add onion and stir until lightly browned. Add the other ingredients in the order listed, then cover and cook over moderate heat for $1^1/_2$ hours. Lift the lid to check whether water is needed. Lower heat so that the dish is kept simmering very gently. Continue cooking until done, about three hours. Slice the beef and serve hot.

FOOD SHOPPING

Although the supermarket concept is the same as in the United States, a quick glance at the shelves reveals that the goods on display are a little different from what is sold in North America. Milk, for example, comes in clear plastic sacks; dishwashing liquid is actually a yellow paste in a pail. Items that are available in the United States in many different brands and flavors, such as salad dressing, are available in Israel.

However, some Israelis never even go to the supermarket. In nearly every neighborhood there is a little grocery store known as a *makolet* (mah-KOH-let), which opens as early as 7 A.M. Usually family-owned, the *makolet* sells many things, from fresh rolls to dairy products, and a nice variety of sundries. There is a warm, friendly atmosphere at the *makolet*, and many choose to do their shopping in what is considered by some to be the neighborhood social center.

The open-air market, or *shuk*, is also a vital part of the Israeli shopping experience. Most towns have a *shuk*, where fruit and vegetables are offered at very reasonable prices. Vendors from all the stalls compete with one another, yelling the prices and benefits of their goods.

ISRAELI SALAD

The most well-known national dish of Israel is the Israeli Salad. Distinguished by the tiny diced tomatoes and cucumbers and refreshing oil and lemon dressing, this is a standard on the table of Israelis from all ethnic groups. The traditional version is usually made as an accompaniment to the main dish at dinnertime. This recipe serves six people.

2 large tomatoes
2 medium cucumbers, peeled
1 green pepper
1 scallion, finely minced
$^1/_2$ avocado (optional)
$^1/_4$ cup oil

$2^1/_2$ tablespoons lemon juice
2 cloves garlic, finely minced
1 tablespoon Italian parsley, finely chopped
$^1/_2$ teaspoon salt
pepper to taste

Dice the tomatoes, green pepper, and cucumbers (and avocado for a slightly richer salad) into $^1/_2$-inch cubes. Mix the tomatoes, cucumbers, green pepper, and scallion in a large bowl. Mix the oil, lemon juice, garlic, parsley, salt, and pepper in a smaller bowl to make the salad dressing. Mix the dressing into the diced vegetables. Serve at room temperature, or refrigerate and serve cold.

JERUSALEM KUGEL

Kugel is a pudding of noodles, eggs, and oil that originated in Eastern Europe. The savory variation of kugel, which usually accompanies the main meal during the sabbath and Jewish festivals, has vegetables and may include potatoes or *challah* as the base. The sweeter version has fruit and sugar or juice; it is eaten as a dessert. This Israeli version of kugel has the unique flavor of caramelized sugar. This recipe serves eight people.

4 quarts (4.5 litres) water
12 ounces (340 g) thin egg noodles
8 tablespoons vegetable oil
1/3 cup sugar

3 eggs, lightly beaten
1 tablespoon salt
pepper to taste
1/3 cup raisins (optional)

Add a little salt to the water in a large pot, and boil. Slowly add the noodles to the boiling water, and cook for six minutes. Drain away all the water, then add two tablespoons of the oil. Mix well, then set aside. Heat the remaining oil with the sugar in a small saucepan over a slow flame for 20 minutes, until the sugar melts and browns. Pour the caramelized sugar over the noodles. Mix well, then leave to cool. Lightly beat the eggs with a little salt and pepper, and add the mixture to the noodles. Add raisins for more sweetness. Transfer the noodles to a nine-inch (23 cm) baking dish, and cover with aluminum foil. Bake in oven preheated to 350°F (177°C) for an hour. For a more traditional kugel with a deeper color, bake for 10 hours overnight at 200°F (93°C). Serve hot.

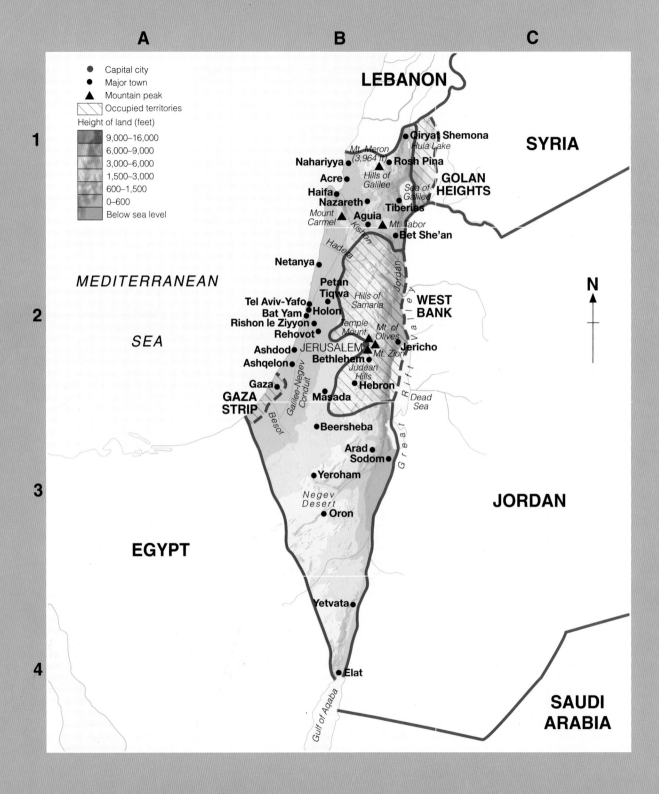

MAP OF ISRAEL

ECONOMIC ISRAEL

Manufacturing

Cement		Light Industry	
Chemicals		Metal processing	
Food processing		Petroleum Refining	
Heavy Industry		Textiles	

Services

Airport   Tourism

Port/ Shipbuilding

Natural Resources

Copper		Phosphate	
Gypsum		Salt	
Oil/Gas			

ABOUT THE ECONOMY

GROSS DOMESTIC PRODUCT
US$119 billion (2001)

LAND AREA
3,029 square miles (20,325 square km)

LAND USE
Arable land 17 percent, permanent crops 4 percent, other 79 percent

AGRICULTURAL PRODUCTS
Citrus fruit, vegetables, cotton, beef, poultry, dairy products

LABOR FORCE
2.4 million (2000)

UNEMPLOYMENT RATE
9 percent (2001)

INFLATION RATE
1.1 percent (2002)

CURRENCY
1 Israel new shekel (ILS) = 100 agorot
1 agora = 10 shekalim
USD1 = ILS4.58 (April 2003)
Notes: 20, 50, 100, 200 new shekel
Coins: 1, 5, 10 agorot; $^{1}/_{2}$, 1, 5, 10 shekalim

MAJOR EXPORTS
Cut diamonds, software, medical and scientific equipment, electronic components, computers, chemicals, agricultural products, textiles, apparel

MAJOR IMPORTS
Diamonds, machinery and equipment, fuel

MAJOR TRADE PARTNERS
Belgium, Germany, Hong Kong, Luxembourg, Netherlands, United Kingdom, United States

PORTS AND HARBORS
Ashdod, Ashqelon, Elat, Hadera, Haifa, Tel Aviv-Yafo

AIRPORTS
Ben Gurion, Ben Yaakov, Elat-J Hozman, Haifa-U Michaeli, Sde Dov

TOURIST ARRIVALS
862,300 (2002)

INTERNATIONAL PARTICIPATION
International Bank for Reconstruction and Development (IBRD); International Criminal Police Organization (Interpol); International Fund for Agricultural Development (IFAD); International Monetary Fund (IMF); International Organization for Standardization (ISO); United Nations (UN); United Nations Educational, Scientific, and Cultural Organization (UNESCO); United Nations High Commissioner for Refugees (UNHCR); United Nations Industrial Development Organization (UNIDO); World Health Organization (WHO)

CULTURAL ISRAEL

Baha'i Gardens
The holiest site of the Baha'i faith in Haifa marks the tomb of the founder of the faith, the prophet Baha'ullah.

Haifa Museums
Consists of three branches, including the Tikotin Museum of Japanese Art, the National Maritime Museum, and the Haifa Musem of Art.

Old Yafo
Ancient ruins stand alongside a modern urban area filled with galleries, shops, cafés, and restaurants in Tel Aviv-Yafo.

Kikar Habimah
This major cultural center houses the Habimah National Theater, the Mann Auditorium (home of the Israeli Philharmonic Orchestra), the Helena Rubinstein Pavilion, and the Gan Ya'akov garden.

Tel Aviv Museum of Art
A world-renowned museum that houses Israeli and international art known for its Impressionist and post-Impressionist collections.

Ruins of Masada
The mountaintop remains of the Roman king Herod's palace fortress in Masada. One thousand Jews committed mass suicide in their failed revolt against the Romans in A.D. 70.

The Negev
The desert region houses craters, valleys, gorges, and mountains. Contains Makhtesh Ramon, the largest natural crater, and Timna Mountains, where King Solomon mined copper.

Eilat (Red Sea)
The most popular tourist city in Israel, located near the sea in the southern tip of Israel.

The Western Wall
Part of the Second Temple complex built by Herod in Jerusalem, this is the remaining wall that was built around the Temple.

Dome of the Rock
An Islamic shrine built in A.D. 691 on the site of the First and Second Jewish Temples.

Church of the Holy Sepulcher
Christianity's holiest site was built in A.D. 330 and contains the location of Jesus' crucifixion, entombment, and resurrection.

El Aqsa Mosque
Islam's third most important place of worship, built in A.D. 720.

Church of the Nativity
This church in Bethlehem marks Jesus' birthplace.

Dead Sea
This lake is the lowest place on earth. The water is so salty that people can stay afloat without any effort.

Tomb of the Patriarchs
The tomb in Hebron is the burial site of Abraham, Isaac, and Jacob and their wives Sarah, Rebecca, and Leah.

The Bedouin Market
Held every Thursday in Beersheva, this market offers ethnic handicrafts such as embroidered clothing, rugs, camel bags, bracelets, amulets, beads, copperware, and coffee pots and mugs.

ABOUT
THE CULTURE

OFFICIAL NAME
State of Israel

NATIONAL FLAG
White, with a blue six-pointed star (Shield of David) centered between two equal horizontal blue bands near the top and bottom edges of the flag

NATIONAL ANTHEM
HaTikvah (The Hope). Written in 1886 by Naftali Herz Imber. Adopted as the nation's anthem in 1948. The lyrics include the words "Our hope will not be lost, the hope of two thousand years, to be a free nation in our land, the land of Zion and Jerusalem."

CAPITAL
Jerusalem. Israel proclaimed Jerusalem as its capital in 1950. However, the United States, like most other countries, maintains its embassy in Tel Aviv.

OTHER MAJOR CITIES
Tel Aviv and Haifa

POPULATION
6,029,529 (2002 est.)

LITERACY RATE
95 percent

ETHNIC GROUPS
Jewish 80.1 percent (Europe/U.S.-born 32.1 percent, Israel-born 20.8 percent, Africa-born 14.6 percent, Asia-born 12.6 percent); non-Jewish (mostly Arab) 19.9 percent

RELIGIOUS GROUPS
Jewish 80.1 percent; Muslim (mostly Sunni Muslim) 14.6 percent; Christian 2.1 percent; other 3.2 percent

OFFICIAL LANGUAGES
Hebrew is the official language; Arabic is used officially for the Arab minority; English is the most commonly used foreign language.

NATIONAL HOLIDAYS
Independence Day. Israel declared independence on May 14, 1948, but following the Jewish lunar calendar the holiday may fall in April or May.

LEADERS IN POLITICS
David Ben-Gurion—first prime minister (1948–54, 1955–63)
Chaim Weizmann—first president (1949–52)
Teddy Kollek—mayor of Jerusalem (1965–93)
Golda Meir—prime minister (1969–74)
Yitzhak Rabin—prime minister (1974–77, 1992–96)
Shimon Peres—prime minister (1984–86, 1995–96)
Ariel Sharon—prime minister since 2001

LEADERS IN THE ARTS
Yehuda Amichai (poet), Paul Ben-Chaim (composer), Ofra Haza (singer), Itzhak Perlman (musician), Amos Oz (writer), Reuven Rubin (painter), Boris Schatz (sculptor), Yehoshua Sobol (playwright)

TIME LINE

IN ISRAEL	IN THE WORLD

13th century B.C.
Exodus from Egypt. Torah and the Ten
Commandments received at Mount Sinai.

722–720 B.C.
Assyrians exile ten Israeli tribes.

753 B.C.
Rome is founded.

116–17 B.C.
The Roman empire reaches its greatest
extent, under Emperor Trajan (98–117).

A.D. 73
Last stand of Jews at Masada.

A.D. 600
Height of Mayan civilization

1000
The Chinese perfect gunpowder
and begin to use it in warfare.

1530
Beginning of trans-Atlantic slave trade
organized by the Portuguese in Africa

1558–1603
Reign of Elizabeth I of England

1620
Pilgrims sail the *Mayflower* to America.

1776
U.S. Declaration of Independence

1789–99
French Revolution

1860
The first neighborhood, Mishkenot
Sha'ananim, is built outside Jerusalem's walls.

1861
U.S. Civil War begins.

1869
The Suez Canal is opened.

1882–1903
First Aliyah, mainly from Russia

1897
Zionist Organization is founded.

1914
World War I begins.

1939–45
World War II; Holocaust in Europe

1939
World War II begins.

1948
State of Israel is declared;
Arab countries attack.

1945
The United States drops atomic bombs
on Hiroshima and Nagasaki.

IN ISRAEL	IN THE WORLD

1949

Egypt, Jordan, Syria, and Lebanon sign a ceasefire agreement. Israel becomes the 59th UN member.

1952

Israel participates in the Olympic Games (in Helsinki) for the first time.

1967

Israel wins Six-Day War.

1968–73

Egypt's War of Attrition against Israel

1973

Yom Kippur War

1978

Israel and Egypt sign Camp David Accords; Prime Minister Begin and Egyptian President Sadat win Nobel Peace Prize.

1982

Israel invades Lebanon.

1987

Intifada in Israel-administered areas

1994

Israel pulls out from Jericho and Gaza and signs peace treaty with Jordan. Rabin, Peres, and Arafat win the Nobel Peace Prize for their efforts toward peace in the Middle east.

1995

Further Israeli withdrawals from the West Bank. Prime Minister Rabin is assassinated at a peace rally. Palestinian self-government widens in the West Bank and the Gaza Strip.

1949

North Atlantic Treaty Organization (NATO) is formed.

1957

Russians launch Sputnik.

1966–69

Chinese Cultural Revolution

1986

Nuclear power disaster at Chernobyl in Ukraine

1991

Break-up of the Soviet Union

1997

Hong Kong is returned to China.

2001

World population surpasses 6 billion; Terrorists crash planes in New York, Washington, D.C., and Pennsylvania.

2003

War in Iraq

GLOSSARY

aliyah (ah-lee-YUH)
Waves of Jewish immigrants to Israel; literally means "going up."

Ashkenazim (AHSH-kuh-NAH-zim)
Jews from northern and eastern Europe.

diaspora
The dispersion of Jews after the Babylonian (587 B.C.) and Roman (A.D. 132) conquests of Palestine.

Histadrut (hiss-tahd-root)
The General Federation of Labor, Israel's most important workers' union.

Holocaust
The killing of six million European Jews by the Nazis during World War II.

Intifada (IN-tuh-FAH-duh)
Civil disobedience and unrest started in 1987 by Palestinian Arabs to protest Israeli occupation of the West Bank and the Gaza Strip.

kibbutz (key-BOOTZ)
A collective farm where people work and live together, sharing all their possessions.

kibbutznik (key-BOOTZ-nik)
Residents of the *kibbutz*.

menorah (muh-noh-ruh)
The seven-branched candelabrum of traditional Jewish worship; the official Israeli emblem.

Palestine
Historically, the area between the Jordan river and the Mediterranean Sea in which most of the biblical narrative is located.

rabbi
A spiritual leader of a Jewish congregation.

sabbath
The seventh day of the week (Saturday), set aside by the Fourth Commandment for rest and worship and observed as such by Jews.

sabra
Nickname for Israelis derived from the name of a cactus fruit that is tough outside but sweet inside.

Sephardim (suh-FAR-dim)
Jews from Aegean, Mediterranean, Balkan, and Middle Eastern countries.

shofar (show-fahr)
A ram's horn, used in ancient times in religious ceremonies as a signal in battle.

ulpan (ool-PAHN)
An institute specially designed to teach Jewish immigrants about the culture of Israel and to offer Hebrew-language lessons.

Zionism
The effort of the Jews to regain and retain their biblical homeland, based on God's promise in the Bible that Israel would belong to the Jews.

FURTHER INFORMATION

BOOKS

Altman, Linda Jacobs. *The Creation of Israel*. California: Lucent Books, 1998.

Blaine, Marge. *Dvora's Journey*. New York: Holt, Rinehart, and Winston, 1976.

Finkelstein, Norman H. *Friends Indeed: The Special Relationship of Israel and the United States*. Connecticut: Millbrook Press, 1998.

Hurwitz, Johanna. *The Rabbi's Girls*. New York: Harper Collins, 1982.

Katz, Mordechai. *Understanding Judaism*. New York: Artscroll Messorah, 2000.

Levine, Anna. *Running on Eggs*. Illinois: Cricket Books, 1999.

Levitin, Sonia. *The Singing Mountain*. New York: Simon & Schuster, 2000.

Schlesinger, Arthur M. and Fred L. Israel (editors). *Jerusalem and the Holy Land: Chronicles from National Geographic*. Pennsylvania: Chelsea House Publisher, 1999.

Schroeter, Daniel J. *Israel: An Illustrated History*. North Carolina: Oxford University Press Children's Books, 1999.

Shalant, Phyllis. *Shalom, Geneva Peace*. New York: Dutton Children's Books, 1992.

Stavsky, Lois (contributor) and I.E. Mozeson. *Jerusalem Mosaic: Young Voices from the Holy City*. New York: Simon & Schuster, 1995.

WEBSITES

Official website of the Israeli government. www.knesset.gov.il

Ha'aretz Daily Newspaper (English-language version). www.haaretzdaily.com

Jerusalem Post (English-language newspaper). www.jpost.com

iGuide (comprehensive index of websites in Israel). www.iguide.co.il

Live radio, news, sports, and arts from Israel. www.kolisrael.com

Israeli portals: www.ynet.co.il; www.walla.co.il; www.start.co.il; www.nana.co.il

VIDEOS

50 Years War: Israel & The Arabs. PBS Home Video, 2000.

Israel: A Nation Is Born. Home Vision Entertainment, 2002.

Exodus. Metro-Goldwyn-Mayer, Inc., 1960.

Sallah. Palisades International Corporation, 1964.

Yentl. Metro-Goldwyn-Mayer, Inc., 1983.

A Life Apart. First Run Features, 1997.

The Sorrow and the Pity. Milestone Pictures, 1972

Minyan in Kaifeng. Gorp Brothers Productions, 2002.

BIBLIOGRAPHY

Eban, Abba. *Personal Witness: Israel Through My Eyes*. New York: G.P. Putnam's Sons, 1992.

Feinstein, Steve. *Israel in Pictures*. Minneapolis: Lerner Publications, 1989.

Grossman, David. *Sleeping on a Wire: Conversations with Palestinians in Israel*. New York: Farrar, Straus and Giroux, 1993.

Harper, Paul. *The Arab-Israeli Conflict*. New York: Bookwright Press, 1990.

Hellander, Paul, Andrew Humphreys, and Neil Tilbury. *Israel & the Palestinian Territories*. (4th ed.) Melbourne: Lonely Planet Publishers, 1999.

Metz, Helen Chapin (editor). *Israel, a Country Study*. Washington, D.C.: U.S. Government Printing Office, 1990.

Rabinovich, Abraham. *Israel*. London: Flint River Press Ltd, 1989.

Reich, Bernard and Gershon Kieval. *Israel, Land of Tradition and Conflict*. Boulder: Westview Press, 1993.

Ullian, Robert. *Frommer's Israel, 3rd Edition*. John Wiley & Sons, 2000.

Winter, Dick. *Culture Shock! Israel*. Portland: Graphic Arts, 1992.

Wright, Martin and Paul Cossali. *Israel and the Palestinians*. Harlow: Longman, 1989.

Fodor's Israel. (5th ed.) New York: Fodor's Travel Publishers, 2001.

A guide to Israel. www.campsci.com/iguide

Airports. www.azworldairports.com/index.htm

Central Intelligence Agency World Factbook webpage on Israel. www.cia.gov/cia/publications /factbook/geos/is.html

Economic and current affairs news updates. www.economist.com/countries/Israel

Embassy of Israel in Washington, D.C. www.israelemb.org

Government website on environmental issues. In Hebrew. www.environment.gov.il

Israel, a country study. http://lcweb2.loc.gov/frd/cs/iltoc.html

Israel and the Palestinian territories. www.lonelyplanet.com/destinations/middle_east /israel_and_the_palestinian_territories

Israel Ministry of Foreign Affairs. www.israel-mfa.gov.il

Israel Ministry of Tourism. www.goisrael.com

Local guide for tourists. www.inisrael.com

Maps of Israel. www.geocities.com/gemiio/Maps_Israel.html

National and religious information. www.amichai.com

News updates. www.virtualjerusalem.com

Official information about the country. www.lincon.com/travel/europe/isreal.htm#trans

Ports & Railways Authority. www.israports.org.il

Travel guide to destinations worldwide. www.fodors.com

Travel guide to places all over the world. www.frommers.com

Various topics about the country. www.stateofisrael.com

INDEX